PRAGUE

PRAGUE

brief characteristics ● points of interest ● walks through the city ● practical information

ISBN 80-7033-400-2

CONTENTS

DISCOVERING THE CITY

Prague (Praha) – the capital city of the Czech Republic, is rightly regarded as one of the most beautiful towns in Europe. The styles of all historical periods as revealed in the architecture are proof of its rich and famous history.

The very setting of Prague adds to its uniqueness: the town grew up in the basin of the longest Bohemian river, the Vltava, and gradually came to cover the surrounding hill–slopes and plateaux. A walk through the narrow streets of the historic centre, along the embankments, across the bridges and in the lively pedestrian zone offers ever new views and impressions.

Prague has 1 217 000 inhabitants, 12 per cent of the entire republic, the largest population of all the towns in the Czech Republic. On its area of 497 sq. km, the density of population is 2 449 persons per sq. km. Prague is the political, commercial, administrative and cultural centre of the country and the seat of the President, the Czech Government and Parliament. On its territory are to be found a number of important industrial plants, especially engineering works and food processing. Prague is the centre of banking, the seat of the major corporations, the main road, rail and air transport junction of the country. In the sphere of culture Prague is home to the best–known theatres, orchestras, the largest museums and art galleries. It is the centre of scientific research and education (Charles University, the Czech University of Technology). The ancient core of Prague has been declared a Historical Town Reserve and a UNESCO World Heritage Site, but there are also modern buildings and extensive housing developments along the rim of the town. The new system of transportation based on a network of Metro lines has provided easy access to even remote parts of the city.

Administratively Prague is divided into 15 districts. The most important monuments are to be found in Prague 1, which is the cultural and commercial centre of the City. It is the destination of foreign visitors, who are attracted to Prague as a renowned European tourist centre.

5th cent.	Arrival of the Slavs on the territory of present day Prague
Last quarter of 9th cent.	Foundation of a prince's hill–fort, the future Prague Castle
First half of 10th cent.	A hill–fort is established on present–day Vyšehrad hill
After 925	Foundation of the Rotunda of St Vitus at Prague Castle
973	Establishment of the Prague bishopric; foundation of a Benedictine Convent at the Church of St George
1070	Foundation of the Vyšehrad Chapter
1168	Construction of the stone–built Judith Bridge
c. 1234	Fortification of the Old Town of Prague, town status granted
1257	Foundation of a second Prague town, the present Lesser Town
1344	The Prague bishopric is raised to archbishopric; foundation stone of St Vitus' Cathedral laid
1346–1378	Prague is the residential town of the Court of Emperor Charles IV and one of the largest town in Europe
1348	Foundation of the first university in Central Europe (now Charles University) and of the New Town of Prague
1402	Jan Hus preaches in Bethlehem Chapel
1419	Defenestration of the Counsellors from the windows of the New Town Hall
1420	Victorious battles of the Hussite armies on Vitkov Hill and at Vyšehrad
1458	George of Poděbrady elected King of Bohemia at the Old Town Hall
1541	Extensive fire at Prague Castle, in Hradčany and the Lesser Town
1583–1612	The Imperial Court of Rudolph II resides in Prague; accumulation of extensive art collections
1618	Defenestration of the Governors of Bohemia at Prague Castle. Battle of the White Mountain, victory of the Habsburg dynasty
1621	Execution of 27 leaders of the Uprising of the Estates on the Old Town Square
1648	Swedish siege to Prague
1680	Major outbreak of the plague
1707	Foundation of a School of Engineering
1741	Invasion of Prague by French, Saxon and Bavarian troops (War of the Austrian Heritage)
1784	The Towns of Prague linked into one administrative unit – the City of Prague
1786	A Czech Patriotic Theatre opens
1818	Foundation of a Patriotic Museum, the predecessor to the National Museum
1832	Establishment of the first Prague engineering works
1845	The railway line Prague – Vienna starts operation
1848	Meeting of the Slavonic Congress, June uprising, battles on the barricades

Some important dates
in the History of Prague

1866	Decision to demolish the town fortifications – decree issued by Emperor Franz Joseph I
1868	Foundation stone of the National Theatre laid
1882	First Sokol Sports Festival on Sharpshooters' Island
1884	Holešovice and Bubeneč incorporated in Prague
1890	First May Day celebrations in Prague
1891	Jubilee Exhibition
1897	First electric tram
1901	Libeň incorporated in Prague
1918	Proclamation of the Czechoslovak Republic, election of T. G. Masaryk as first President
1922	37 communities linked up to form Greater Prague
1939	Occupation by the Nazi armies, establishment of the Protectorate of Bohemia and Moravia
1942	Assassination of the Reich Protector R. Heydrich
1945	Prague Uprising and liberation by the Red Army
1968	"Prague Spring" forcible brought to an end when the armies of five Warsaw Pact countries invade Czechoslovakia
1974	Prague Metro starts operation
1989	The "Velvet Revolution", end of the dominance of the Communist Party
1993	Czechoslovakia split into two countries, the Czech Republic and Slovakia. Prague remains Capital City of the Czech Republic

St Vitus' Cathedral,
view from the Riding School

Highest elevation – 391 m above sea level, Kopanina
Lowest elevation above sea level – 177 m, northern edge of Prague, where the R. Vltava leaves the city
Highest absolute temperature – 37. 8 ^{o}C, 27 July 1983, Clementinum
Lowest absolute temperature – –27.6 ^{o}C, 1 March 1785, Clementinum
Absolute maximum daily precipitations – 90mm/24 h, 19 July 1981 Clementinum
Greatest flow of the R. Vltava – absolute maximum 4 580 $m^3.s^{-1}$, 28 February 1784
Lowest flow of the R. Vltava – absolute minimum 11.5 $m^3.s^{-1}$, 27 August 1904 (normal flow is c. 150 $m^3.s^{-1}$)
Tallest tower – Telecommmunications tower at Žižkov, 216 m
Highest building – Motokov, 102 m
Highest steeple – St Vitus' Cathedral, 96,6 m
Largest square – Charles Square, 80 550 sq.m.
Largest cemetery – Olšanské hřbitovy, 520 000 sq. m., established 1680
Largest department store – Kotva, 21 000 sq. m. in area
Largest hall – Congress Hall of the Palace of Culture, 2 970 seats

Pragues highest, largest, best

The Astronomical Clock
on the Old Town Hall, detail

Largest library – National Library of the Czech Republic, over 5.5 mil volumes
Largest equestrian statue – Jan Žižka of Trocnov on Žižkov Hill, height 9 m., monument with pedestal 20 m
Largest stadium – Strahov Stadium, internal area 310.5 x 202.5 m
Largest bell – Sigismund, St Vitus' Cathedral, height 203 cm, diameter 256 cm.
Largest clock – on the Church of the Sacred Heart of the Lord on George of Poděbrady Square
Oldest metereological station – Clementinum, uninterrupted measurements since 1775
Oldest guide to Prague – published by M. Martinic in 1615
Oldest embankment – now Smetana Embankment, construction began in 1841
Oldest university – Charles University, founded 1348
Oldest tunnel – Rudolph tunnel linking the R. Vltava with the royal deer park (1583–93)
Most leaning tower – Šítkov water tower, leaning 68 cm from perpendicularity
Longest street – Plzeňská, 10.5 km
Shortest street – Boršov, 40 m
Oldest railway station – Ferdinand Station, now Masaryk Station, 1845
Most universal time–piece – Old Town Astronomical Clock

The National Monument
on Žižkov Hill

First self–service catering establishment – Koruna, Wenceslas Square (1910–13)
First telephone directory – 1883, 100 subscribers
First street with pavement – now Železná, 1803
First regular refuse collection – 1681
First maternity home – 1762, founded by Empress Maria Theresa
First numbering of houses – 1770
First city power station – 1889 at Žižkov
First football grounds – 1889 on the Imperial Meadow
First asphalt roadway – 1920
Oldest carillon – Loreta, dated 1694
First coffee–house – At the Golden Serpent, 1708, established by Georgius Destatus
First pawn shop – 1747, At the Golden Lion on Lesser Town Square

THE RIVER VLTAVA IN PRAGUE

In fairly recent geological time the River Vltava changed its course and instead of flowing into the Danube began to turn north. On the territory of what is now Prague it formed a riverbed 100m. deep, which, together with a number of tributaries, shaped the face of present–day Prague.

From the beginning the river facilitated settlement and crafts activities. Weirs, mills, water towers began to be built. The inhabitants – fishermen, rafters, sandmen, ferry-men, ice–men and others – won their livelihood from the river. As technical knowl-edge improved, water power began to be put to use and saw–mills, grinding-mills, tanning works, paper works, bleaching plants and calico works came into existence along the banks. The river eased the transport of timber, salt and other raw materi-als essential for the development of the flourishing town, but it retarded the even de-velopment of both banks. Before the bridges were built, people had to cross the river at fords or by ferry–boats. There were three ferries: the upper where today J. Mánes Bridge stands, the middle ferry led across Sharpshooters' Island, and the lower, at Podskalí, went to and fro where Palacký Bridge is today. When Judith Bridge collapsed, a new one, Charles Bridge, was built, and others followed later. The river caused a great deal of worry. Frequent floods inundated a considerable part of Prague, the Old Town, the Lesser Town and mainly Josefov. For long centu-ries the banks kept being strengthened to prevent the water from penetrating deep into the town. In 1841 a first section was built up along the Old Town bank, where Smetana Embankment stretches today. Next came the section between Charles Bridge and the present House of Artists (1875–1877). In an endeavour to win new space for the growing town the embankments were widened into the river. This amounted to as much as 27 m where Dvořák Embankment is today and as much as 50m. at the present Rašín Embankment. The construction of the embankments and apartment houses involved the demolition of the old village of Podskalí, the home of fishermen, rafters and timber–workers, which used to lie between Vyšehrad and Palacký Bridge.

The need to increase trade downstream led to plans to make the Vltava navigable. Until that time only the port at Karlín of 1822 had been available to river boats. In

The River Vltava
in Prague

1895 the port at Holešovice began operation, four years later the Smíchov rafters' port began to be built, and work started on a lock at Štvanice in 1907. The waterway was completed by 1920. In this century the Vltava was bound by a series of dams, the "Vltava Cascade". In Prague the river is enclosed between stone embankments, and it is used by excursion boats as well as tug–boats. Nowadays few people remember that the Vltava was the cradle of certain aquatic sports. The first canoes and rowing boats in Bohemia were used here, and in winter the river would freeze over, and people went skating on the ice.

THE ISLANDS

Over the centuries the R. Vltava formed many islands: some vanished again during floods while others rose above the waters. Towards the end of the 18th cent. the people of Prague began to build up the banks, and thereby they gained new land literally in the centre of the town. Many important events have taken place on these islands. The southernmost of the islands is **Imperial Meadow** (Císařská louka). Somewhere in this area King Václav II held his coronation banquet in 1297. The island itself was shaped by floodwaters in 1890. On that occasion the rafts anchored on the Podskalí banks opposite were torn away and partly blocked the current below the pillars of Charles Bridge. Two of these pillars and three arches collapsed. For that reason a raft harbour was built at Smíchov in 1899–1903, in which rivercraft could find anchorage. The harbour protected the rafts at times of floodwater and served, furthermore, as a transfer area for timber. This harbour cut the Imperial

A pleasure steamer
on the R. Vltava

Meadow off from the Smíchov bank and created an artificial island. The harbour can be approached from the north and the south and is roughly 1 400m. in length. A stadium for aquatic sports, boat–houses and a campsite are to be found on the island.

Across the river from Imperial Meadow, on the Podolí bank, between the swimming stadium and the Podolí waterworks, lies **Oarsmen's Island** (Veslařský ostrov), where the rowing clubs have their boathouses.

Slavonic Island (Slovanský ostrov) came into existence by alluvial deposits in the 18th cent. Walls were built to contain it, and trees were planted. Public baths were set up, and a leather dye work was in operation. In 1830 the Prague miller Novotný had a Neo–Renaissance building with a ballroom built there, at the time the largest in Prague. Nowadays, after extensive reconstruction, the building is used for cultural purposes. At its southern end stands the Šítkov Tower and the Mánes exhibition hall, at the northern end a statue of writer B. Němcová is to be found.

Not far from Slavonic Island, closer to the Smíchov side, lies **Sharpshooters' Island** (Střelecký ostrov). In 1472 a sharpshooters' shooting range was set up here, and in 1812 a building was erected for the Corps of Prague Sharpshooters. A few years later an army swimming pool was opened at the northern point. In June 1882 the Sokol Sports Festival was held on the island on the occasion of the twentieth anniversary of the Prague Sokol Association. The mass gymnastic performances were directed by the founder of the Sokol Movement, Dr. M. Tyrš, in person.

The long **Children's Island** (Dětský ostrov) stretches along the Smíchov bank. It was formerly known as Jew Island after the Jewish owner of a cotton printing mill that stood on the island in the 19th cent. The island has a large children's playground, and at its northern end stands a statue of the River Vltava, where every year wreaths are placed in memory of the drowned.

Kampa Island is separated from the Lesser Town by the Čertovka, which was a millrace for three mills. Until the second half of the 16th cent. Kampa Island was one large garden. At that time two rows of little houses were built, which still stand on the site. In the area between them potters' markets have been held since 1599, and the tradition has been re–established. The park on the island is an oasis of quiet, and from the embankment there is an interesting view across the river to the Old Town. A small house opposite Lichtenstein Palace once belonged to J. Dobrovský, one of the men responsible for the Czech National Revival last century.

Štvanice Island lies where a ford crossed the river on the route to the north. In 1889 the depth of the river here was 75 cm. In the 14th century there used to be vegetable gardens on these islands, later a shooting range and in the 18th cent. a stockade was built in which wild animals were chased, from which the island derives its name (štvanice = the chase). There were also fairground attractions until trees were planted in the 19th cent. The most important changes in the course of the river took place early this century when the river was made navigable, and locks were built. In the western part of the island a hydro–electric power station was built in 1912–1913, which, since reconstruction, again supplies almost one third of electric energy to light the city. There is a winter stadium on the island with the oldest ice-rink in Prague. It was opened in 1932 and became the venue of the Ice Hockey World Championship in 1933. The central part of the island is taken up by tennis courts with a Central Court. Štvanice Island is the only one of the Prague islands crossed by two bridges, Hlávka

Bridge and the Negrelli railway bridge. Below it, under the river, runs Line C of Prague Metro.

Down river used to lie two other islands (Rohan and Libeň Islands) – but all that remains after the building of the Port of Prague are their names since they were joined to the mainland.

The last and most northerly island on the territory of Prague is **Imperial Island** (Císařský ostrov), of which Troja Island (Trojský ostrov) now forms a part. It was artificially created when the Canal for Troja lock was built in 1899–1902. In 1927 a race ground was laid out on the island, and a second canal was used for competitions in shooting the rapids.

THE BRIDGES ACROSS THE R. VLTAVA

In the earliest days people who wished to cross the R. Vltava used fords or ferries. In the 10th cent. there is mention of a wooden bridge. Two hundred years later Judith Bridge was finished; after its destruction by floodwater in 1342 Emperor Charles IV had a new stone bridge built, which bears his name, Charles Bridge. No other bridges were built across the river until the thirties of the 19th cent. when industry developed.

The southernmost of the Prague bridges is **Peace Race Bridge** (most Závodu míru), constructed 1961–1964. It is widely used by motorists crossing from Zbraslav to the right bank or in the opposite direction. It is almost 8 km to the next road bridge across the Vltava.

The Braník Railway Bridge (Branický železniční most, 1950–1955) links the railway stations Praha–Krč and Praha–Chuchle; it has a footway for pedestrians.

Barrandov Bridge (Barrandovský most, 1978–1988) is a major bridge providing a road link between Brno, Prague and Plzeň (and Strakonice). It facilitates public transport for people living on the right bank in the southern parts of Prague to Line B of Prague Metro.

Prague
Bridges

The Vyšehrad Railway Bridge (Vyšehradský železniční most, 1900–1901) was built on pillars of an older bridge. It has a pedestrian footway. The bridge provides a link between the Praha–Smíchov railway station and the Main Station (Hlavní nádraží) and the Praha–Vršovice station. Below the bridge the little river Botič flows into the Vltava.

Palacký Bridge (most Palackého, 1876–1878). At the bridge ends used to stand groups of statues by J. V. Myslbek, which were partly damaged during an air–raid in 1945. They are now to be seen at Vyšehrad.

Jirásek Bridge (Jiráskův most, 1929–1933) crosses the Vltava in front of the windows where A. Jirásek, a Czech novelist, lived from 1903 to 1930. The bridge is an important thoroughfare between Smíchov and the New Town. Between Palacký and Jirásek bridges is the quay from which the Vltava pleasure steamers depart.

Legion Bridge (most Legií, 1898–1901) now stands where the first chain bridge in Prague used to be. The winning project for the bridge was exhibited at the Jubilee Exhibition im 1891.

Charles Bridge (Karlův most). For the detailed description and plan see p. 73 ff.

Mánes Bridge (most Josefa Mánesa, 1911–1914) links Jan Palach Square with Klárov.

Čech Bridge (Čechův most, 1905–1908) is a continuation of Pařížská Street, built on the pattern of the Paris bridges. It has a wrought iron construction with rich sculptural decorations.

During reconstruction of the Letná bridge–end in 1950 the Chapel of St Mary Magdalene was moved 31 m.

Šverma Bridge (Švermův most, 1949–1951) is an extension of Revoluční Street to the Letná side and leads to a 429 m. long road tunnel that ends at Letná. The bridge was built on the site of another chain bridge.

Hlávka Bridge (Hlávkův most, 1906–1012) links Těšnov with Holešovice via Štvanice Island. Its construction is, among others, due to the establishment of the slaughterhouse at Holešovice at the end of last century (now Holešovice market). The bridge was reconstructed in 1971–1975 and forms part of the North–South Freeway.

The Karlín Railway Bridge (Karlínský železniční most, 1846–1850, Negrelli viaduct) was the longest railway structure in Europe in its day (Length 1 130 m.). After Charles Bridge it is the second longest bridge still in use. At the time of its construction the bridge had 85 arches and linked the present Masaryk Station with Bubny Station on the line to Dresden. The viaduct was designed by A. Negrelli and J. Perner, Negrelli being one of the planners of the Corinth Canal and the Suez Canal. The viaduct can be clearly seen from the river and from the bus terminal Praha–Florenc.

Libeň Bridge (Libeňský most, 1925–1928) leads across Libeň Island and the Port of Prague. It links Holešovice with Libeň.

The Railway Bridge (Železniční most, 1967–1975) is part of the line to Holešovice Junction; it was built to shorten the connection between the Prague–Holešovice Railway Station and other stations in the eastern part of Prague.

Barricaders' Bridge (most Barikádníků, 1975–1980) replaced the original Troja Bridge of 1926–1928. It derives its name from the people on the barricades who defended their city in the May 1945 uprising. The older bridge had to give way in view of the heavy traffic on the North–South Freeway.

---

*The Bridges across
the R. Vltava*

The tramway bridge (Most elektrické dráhy, 1974–1976) provides a link for trams running between Holešovice and Troja, Kobylisy and Ďáblice.
The footbridge from Imperial Island to Troja (Zoo, Troja chateau) and Stromovka Park gives the possibility of pleasant walks in this quiet part of Prague.

PRAGUE TOWERS

The attribute of Prague as a City of a Hundred Spires is no longer true. It is not easy to count all the towers, but it is claimed that there are more than 500. These towers served various purposes, some added beauty to ecclesiastical buildings and supported bells; others were of defensive character, a few were used to pump water for distribution to the town. And present–day towers bear television aerials.

St Vitus' Cathedral at Prague Castle has three tall towers. The highest rises to 96.6 m. Its bells can be heard from afar, and thanks to Prague Radio they resound in all corners of the republic. Open to the public under favourable weather conditions.

The other towers of Prague Castle shape the panorama of Prague, particularly the **towers of the Romanesque church of St George,** and the **Daliborka,** the **Black** and the **White Towers.**

The Powder Tower (Prašná brána) rises to 65 m. It stands on the site of its predecessor, the Tattered Tower. At one period it was a storehouse of gun powder, hence its name. There is a gallery high up the tower that is open to the public and opens up an interesting view over the city.

The Church of Our Lady before Týn (kostel P. Marie před Týnem), known for short as Týn Church, towers above the Old Town Square. The early 16th century towers rise to 70 m, the southern tower is broader, the northern one was renovated in 1825 after being gutted by fire in 1819.

The tower of the Old Town Hall (height 69.5 m) had its foundation stone laid in 1364 and was probably completed in 1381. It is the symbol of the Old Town and served as watch tower in case of fire. Its upper gallery is open to the public.

The Astronomical Tower of the Clementinum (Hvězdárenská věž), dating from 1727, bears on its top a statue of the Titan Atlas. The tower itself was built in 1721–1723. Astronomical observations were carried out from there, and since 1775 regular measurements of temperature and air pressure have been recorded as well as other data. The tower was important for the rhythm of life in the town. From 1891 to 1918 a flag was waved from the gallery at midday as a signal for the artillery on the Marian Ramparts, which, by discharging a gun, announced this fact to the whole of Prague.

The Old Town Bridge Tower (Staroměstská mostecká věž) stands at the bridge end of Charles Bridge. It originated in the late 14th and early 15th cent. Experts claim that it is the most beautiful medieval tower in Europe.

The Lesser Town Bridge Towers (Malostranská mostecká věž) stand at the Lesser Town end of Charles Bridge and form a counterpart to the Old Town Bridge Tower. The lower tower dates from the 12th cent., the higher was built in the middle of the 15th cent. It is open to the public.

The Church of St Nicholas (chrám sv. Mikuláše) in the Lesser Town draws attention to itself by its mighty dome which can be seen from afar. By its side stands a narrow, almost 80 m high belfry built in the years 1751–1756.

The New Town Hall (Novoměstská radnice) stands at the northern end of Charles Square. Its tower was built 1451–1456 and is one of the most beautiful in Prague. Open to the public. The New Town Hall is used for cultural events.

The panorama of Prague is framed by the two Neo–Gothic **towers of the Church of SS Peter and Paul at Vyšehrad.** They date from 1902. Two further steeples grace the Church of St Ludmila on Peace Square (náměstí Míru) in Vinohrady. The original towers of the **Abbey Church of the Virgin Mary (Emmaus)** – (kostel P. Marie na Slovanech) damaged in 1945, were replaced by two architecturally striking slim spires in 1967.

The New Town Water Tower (Novoměstská vodárenská věž) was built three times, in 1489, 1588 and 1651. The first was destroyed by fire, and it had to be re–built again after the Swedish bombardment in 1648. Until 1847 water was piped from it to the fountains of the New Town. By its side stood a mill, Šítkov Mill, which ceased operation in 1928.

The Old Town Water Tower (Staroměstská vodárenská věž) was first built in 1489 and again in 1575. Records have survived that show that it burnt down seven times. It served the Old Town and adjacent mills. Its immediate vicinity is known as Novotný's footpath (Novotného lávka), named for miller Novotný. A small metal plaque in the wall of the tower bears the date 4 September 1890 and shows the highest level that the R. Vltava reached during floods at the time. By the tower stand the Old Town mills and the waterworks of the City of Prague, built in 1883 and now used as Smetana Museum.

The New Mill Water Tower (Novomlýnská vodárenská věž) was built in 1536 when the mills were known as "new mills". They were demolished when the Vltava was regulated in 1906–1925. The present appearance of the tower dates from 1658.

The Lesser Town Water Tower (Malostranská vodárenská věž) was built in the middle of the 17th cent. It supplied water to 57 Lesser Town fountains.

Some church steeples suffered a sad fate. They remained on their own or did not reach the same height as their partners. The chief cause used to be fire. At the **Church of St Giles** (kostel sv. Jiljí) the northern tower was destroyed by fire in 1432 and its spire was never completed. At the **Church of St James** (kostel sv. Jakuba) fire destroyed the left tower in 1754. At the **Church of Our Lady Victorious** (kostel P. Marie Vítězné) the northern tower was never finished, for Joseph II dissolved the convent before the Carmelites managed to build the steeple. The **Church of St Saviour** (kostel sv. Salvátora) has only one tower, the **Church of St John of Nepomuk** (kostel sv. Jana Nepomuckého) became an army store and was in such bad repair that the tower had to be partly taken down in 1815.

The Petřín View Tower (Petřínská rozhledna) owes its origin to the Club of Czech Tourists who visited the World Exhibition in Paris in 1889. By collecting contributions from members of the club and other sponsors they undertook the construction, in March 1891, and it was festively opened on 20 August 1891. The height of the tower is 60 m, and its top now bears a TV aerial 20 m in length.

The Telecommunications Tower in Žižkov is the youngest and the highest of the Prague towers. It was constructed in the years 1987–1990. Its base of three joined

tubes supports the TV aerals, raising the tower to the height of 216 m. There is an observation restaurant on the tower.

Green belts are attractive both for the local inhabitants and for visitors. They provide places of rest and promote leisure–time activities. Some localities outside the city centre are Protected Territories where strict rules are enforced. We have selected the best known and most frequently visited as examples:

Petřín Hill is a major area of parkland. From the 12th to the early 19th cent. vines were cultivated on the slopes, and in the western parts the building stone of many Romanesque and Gothic works of Prague architecture was quarried. On the southern slopes Count Kinský had a garden laid out in 1825, now bearing his name, **Kinský**

The Petřín
Tower

The Lesser Town
Bridge Tower

Garden, which was further enlarged in 1848–1860. Gardens then were laid out along the entire eastern slope of Petřín Hill. In 1830 a summer house was built. In 1901 the gardens were purchased by the municipality and in 1929 an old wooden church from Slovakia was transferred to the upper part of the garden.

Kinský Garden is separated from the Petřín Orchards (Petřínské sady) by the Hunger Wall (Hladová zeď). Not far from the View Tower near the planetarium is a **rose garden,** planted in 1930.

Strahov Garden (Strahovská zahrada), which belongs to Strahov Abbey, stretches along the old fortifications. It was laid out in the 17th cent. and adapted in the fifties of the 20th cent.

On the slopes going down to the R. Vltava there are several gardens that bear the names of the original owners.:

The Lobkowicz Garden (Lobkovická zahrada) was laid out on terraces that made use

Green Belts
in the Capital

The T. V. Tower
at Žižkov

of the natural slope of the land. The first rock garden in Bohemia came into existence here.

The Seminary Garden (Seminářská zahrada) belonged to the Carmelite Convent of Our Lady Victorious from the middle of the 17th cent. When the cloister was dissolved, the garden became the property of the archbishops.

Letná Park (Letenské sady) has a long history, beginning with the coronation feast of Přemysl Otakar II that was held here in 1261. Emperor Sigismund camped here with his army after losing the battle at Vítkov in 1420. Nowadays an unusual view of Prague opens up from above Čech Bridge and Pařízská street. The Hanau Pavillion stands close to this spot. It originally was an exhibition hall for the foundries of Prince Hanau, who presented the building to the town after the Jubilee Exhibition in 1891.

From Letná Park it is possible to walk in a westerly direction to **Chotek Park** (Chot-

The Franciscan Garden with the Church
of Our Lady of the Snows

kovy sady). This is one of the oldest parks in Prague. It bears the name of Count K. Chotek, who had it laid out in 1831 on the site of an army training ground and timber store. Even further to the west it links up with the **Royal Garden** (Královská zahrada), laid out in 1534 between Stag Moat (Jelení příkop) and the Marian Ramparts (Mariánské hradby). From its beginning it was planted with exotic trees and plants, which, at the time, included tulips.

Čelakovský Park (Čelakovského sady) near the National Museum was laid out in 1882 before the museum was built. At the present time the North–South Freeway encloses the park on both sides.

Vrchlický Park (Vrchlického sady) originated in 1876 on the site of the former fortifications, demolished in 1874. As early as 1827 Count Chotek had proposed a promenade with three rows of trees along the walls and bastions leading from Horse Gate to Hospice Gate. Now the park provides relaxation for travellers waiting for their trains outside the Main Station

Rieger Park (Riegrovy sady) took the place of an older park that had to give way to building construction in Vinohrady. In 1938 a sports ground with a stadium was built and a garden restaurant opened up.

Žižkov Hill is known for the victorious battle that the Hussites won here in 1420. It provides a good viewpoint and is dominated by the National Memorial, its future to be determined.

Havlíček Park (Havlíčkovy sady) has existed since 1879. There are some artificial caves (19th cent.). Vineyards stretch along the southern slopes.

A small but very pleasant place for a quiet rest is the **Franciscan Garden** (Františkánská zahrada) between Jungmann Square and the Alfa Passage. It first belonged to the Carmelite Order and from the 17th cent. to the Franciscans. Souvenirs are sold in the gazebo in the centre in the midst of a herb garden. In one corner is a small children's playground with a fountain.

The royal deer–park is better known as **Stromovka Park.** Its woodland territory close to the R. Vltava was a hunting ground already during the reign of Přemysl Otakar II and served as such under subsequent monarchs. Rudolph II had a summer palace built, had the lake enlarged and a tunnel built that supplied the lakes with water from the Vltava. In 1804 the park was opened to the public. In 1845 and 1867 two railway lines began to run alongside the park to the north and the south.

Únětice Valley (Únětické údolí) lies at the northern point of the city on the left bank of the Vltava. The Únětice stream runs down the valley and has laid bare schist rocks used by rock climbers as training ground.

The Wild and the Quiet **Šárka** (Divoká a Tichá Šárka) with its romantic scenery is the destination of town dwellers's trips. This has become more attractive since a lake swimming pool called Džbán, was built. The valley forms a narrow rocky gorge lined by broad meadows with meadow flora. On the right bank of the stream, high above the valley, once stood a Slavic hill–fort.

The Star Park (Obora Hvězda) is named after the summer palace with the ground plan of a sixpointed star. It was here in 1620 that the tragic Battle of the White Mountain took place, which the Czech army lost to the imperial armies. Ferdinand I had set up a hunting lodge here in 1534 with walls and two gateways. The main path from the Břevnov gate leads to the Star summer palace, now used as Jirásek and Aleš Museum.

Green Belts
in the Capital

The Procopius and Daleje Valleys (Prokopské a Dalejské údolí) run in a deep cleft in Palaeozoic limestone. Though quarrying was carried on for several centuries, most of the quarries are now overgrown with vegetation and merge with the surroundings. There are interesting geological formations (folds, remnants of submarine volcanoes) and rich thermophile flora of rock–steppe character. A railway line runs through the valley.

Chuchle Wood (Chuchelský háj), formed by thermophile vegetation, stretches along the rocky slopes and the plateau between Malá and Velká Chuchle above the railway line.

Zámky, Čimice and Bohnice Valleys (Zámky, Čimické a Bohnické údolí). The rocky promontory of Zámky was settled already in pre–history (hill–fort), in view of its interesting location. In Čimice Valley there are slopes of schist rock, while grapes used to be grown in the Bohnice Valley. This patch of open ground on the right bank

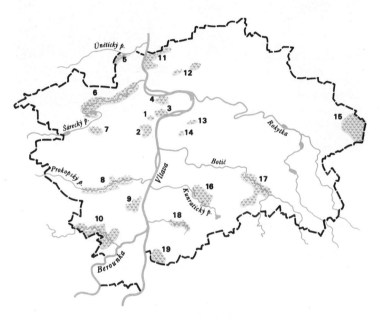

1 Royal Garden
2 Petřín Park
3 Letná Park
4 Stromovka Park
5 Únětice Valley
6 Wild and Quiet Šárka
7 Star Park
8 Procopius and Daleje Valleys
9 Chuchle Woods
10 Radotín Valley

11 Zámky, Čimice and Bohnice Valleys
12 Ďáblice and Čimice Woods
13 Žižkov Hill
14 Rieger Park
15 Klánovice
16 Kunratice and Michle Wood
17 Hostivař and Milíč Wood
18 Modřany Gorge
19 Točná

of the Vltava, where the river leaves the territory of Prague, is used by the inhabitants of the near housing developments. The same is true of the **Ďáblice and Čimice Woods** (Ďáblický a Čimický háj).

Klánovice lies in the most easterly part of the city and is surrounded by woodland stretching along both sides of the railway line Prague–Kolín.

The Kunratice and Michle Wood (Kunratický a Michelský les) with a network of paths provides enjoyment for the inhabitants of the South Town, and not only them. The Kunratice stream flows around a high ridge on which King Václav IV had a New Castle built in 1410–1412, and he died there in 1419. Later the castle was conquered and levelled to the ground by the Hussites. Its ruins can by seen on the top of the ridge. For the last 50 years the area has been the venue of a cross–country running competition.

Hostivař Reservoir (Vodní nádrž Hostivař) on the R. Botič and its environs are an interesting part in close vicinity of modern housing developments. In the valley the Pitkovice stream and the R. Botič form natural meanders with dense undergrowth on the banks and with protected flora. Along the nature trail that runs through the area is the **Milíčovský Wood** with a lake of the same name.

Green Belts
in the Capital

Limestone cliffs
in Procopius Valley

Modřany Gorge (Modřanská rokle) is used by the inhabitants of the new housing developments in the southern part of the city, and the same is true of the environs of **Točná** with Šance summit above the Břežanské valley.

Scenic flights over Prague are operated from the small local air–field.

WALKS THROUGH THE TOWN

Visitors who have only a few days to spend in Prague concentrate their interest on the ancient centre of the capital city. Here are to be found the most important works of architecture, the majority of cultural institutions (theatres, museums, cinemas, concert halls, etc.) and the best shopping facilities (department stores and specialized shops). All traffic routes converge on the centre (the Metro, main line railway stations), and the central bus terminus is not far away. Walks can be taken through the gardens, parks and along the embankments with unforgettable views of the R. Vltava and the sights on both banks of the river. The unique atmosphere of Prague as an ancient historic town in the heart of Europe can best be appreciated by wandering around these parts. A few suggestions are presented in the following pages of this guidebook.

In each historic quarter of the city the most important sights are described giving their exact location. Orientation is made easier by numbers (on blue number plates) that are to be found on each of the buildings mentioned. On the left–hand side of each street, starting from the river, the buildings have odd numbers, those on the right–hand side have even numbers. On a number of buildings there are metal plaques, but not always are the names and dates given in this guide–book identical with them since new facts that have come to light by recent research are reflected in our guidebook.

To make walks through Prague easier three lines of the Metro will take you to your destination. The starting point for people wishing to get to know the historic core of Prague on foot is the pedestrian zone along the **Royal Route** (Královská cesta). The kings of Bohemia progressed along this route during their coronation processions throughout the Middle Ages. The Royal Route begins at the Powder Tower (Prašná brána), follows Celetná Street to the Old Town Square (Staroměstské náměstí) and goes along Karlova Street to Charles Bridge (Karlův most). The Royal Route then continues over the bridge, along Mostecká Street to Lesser Town Square (Malostranské náměstí) and from there uphill along Nerudova Street till it reaches Prague Castle (Pražský hrad). Shopping expeditions are best centred on the **Golden Cross** (Zlatý kříž), i.e. Wenceslas Square (Václavské náměstí), Na příkopě Street, Národní Street, 28. října Street and Jungmann Square (Jungmanovo náměstí), which lie partly in the pedestrian zone.

Prague became one united town in 1784. Until that date the individual parts had developed as separate units.

The dominating features of Prague is **Prague Castle** (Pražský hrad) situated on a promontory above the left bank of the R. Vltava. From the end of the 9th century it was the residence of the rulers of Bohemia, and it is nowadays that of the President of the Republic. Adjacent to it lies Hradčany, a subject town in c. 1320, which received a royal charter in 1598. Below Prague Castle, on the left bank of the R. Vltava,

Walks through the Town

lies the **Lesser Town** (Malá Strana), founded by King Přemysl Otakar II in 1257. The **Old Town** (Staré Město), on the right bank of the river, dates back to the 10th century when scattered settlements existed along the trade route and near the ford that crossed the Vltava. The Old Town grew up slowly around the market centre on the present Old Town Square (Staroměstské náměstí) and along the road to Judith Bridge, built in the 12th century. In 1232 to 1234, under Václav I, this area was fortified with gateways and began to attract settlers. This gave rise to the most important of the Prague towns, the Old Town of Prague (Staré Město Pražské). On its territory was an enclave for Jewish inhabitants, the **Jewish Town** (Židovské Město), which, in 1850, became the Prague quarter of Josefov. In 1348 Emperor Charles IV founded the largest and most densely populated **New Town** (Nové Město) in the immediate vicinity of the Old Town. It was to be a centre of production and trade and in its time its town planning layout was among the most advanced. **Vyšehrad** (the "upper castle") was, for a time in the 11th and 12th centuries, the seat of the Přemyslid rulers, and it became a separate town in 1476. It has been a Prague quarter since 1884.

The pedestrian zone
in Na příkopě street

The most important monument in the capital city, Prague Castle (Pražský hrad), has, for more than a thousand years, been the symbol of the state of Bohemia. Its beginnings go back to the last quarter of the 9th century. A medieval hill-fort founded by the first Christian Přemyslid Prince Bořivoj became the main seat of this ruling dynasty. The growth of the state of Bohemia was directed from here, and the history of Prague Castle is related to this. The first stone building on the hill-fort was the Church of St Mary, built by Prince Bořivoj (before 894); in c. 920 Vratislav I laid the foundation stone to the Church of St George, after 925 Prince Wenceslas founded the Rotunda of St Vitus; in 973 the Prague bishopric was established and had its seat in the grounds of the hill-fort. In the course of the 11th century a Romanesque basilica replaced the Rotunda of St Vitus. In the 12th century Prince Soběslav I changed the clay walls to stone fortifications with several new towers and began to reconstruct the prince's palace in Romanesque style. The Castle became the seat of the monarch when Vladislav II won the right to a hereditary royal crown in 1158. The Castle was further expanded during the reign of

Prague
Castle

View
from Prague Castle

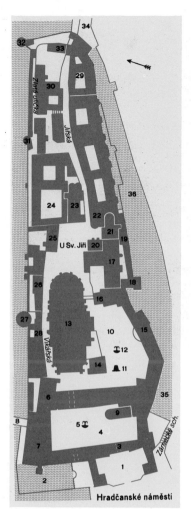

1 The First Courtyard
2 Garden on the Bastion
3 The Matthias Gateway
4 The Second Courtyard
5 Baroque fountain
6 The Rudolph Gallery
7 The Spanish Hall
8 The Dusty Bridge
9 The Holy Rood Chapel
10 The Third Courtyard
11 The monolith
12 The equestrian statue of St George
13 St Vitus' Cathedral
14 The Old Provosts' Palace
15 The Municipal Tract: southern side of the courtyard
16 The Royal Palace
17 Wladislav Hall
18 The Ludwig Wing
19 The Theresian Wing
20 The Old Diet
21 The All Saints' Chapel
22 Rožmberk Palace
23 St George's Basilica
24 St George's Convent
25 The New Provosts' Palace
26 The Old Deanery
27 The Powder (Mihulka) Tower
28 The Vikárka restaurant
29 Lobkowicz Palace
30 The Burgrave's Palace
31 The White Tower
32 The Daliborka Tower
33 The Black Tower
34 Observation terrace
35 The Paradise Garden
36 The Garden on the Ramparts

Charles IV in the 14th century when it became the imperial residence. There was great building activity, including the foundation of the Cathedral of St Vitus in 1344. Building work at the Castle was interrupted in the 15th century when the Kings of Bohemia resided at the Royal Court in the Old Town. The end of the century brought new life to the Castle. Wladislav of Jagiello moved back to the Hradčany Castle in 1484 and initiated its reconstruction in Late Gothic style (Wladislav Hall). In 1526 the Habsburgs ascended the throne of

Bohemia and rebuilt the Castle in Renaissance style (the Summer Palace, the Royal Garden). An extensive fire at the Castle in 1541 left long–term consequences but made new construction possible, which reached its climax during the reign of Rudolph II (1576–1611). Prague Castle became an important centre of the arts and sciences (Rudolph owned a large art collection). In the 17th century with its tempestuous events (1618 Prague Defenestration, 1620 defeat of the Bohemian Estates at the Battle of the White Mountain, the Thirty Years' War) Prague Castle became merely a temporary abode of the Imperial Court, which centred on Vienna. Major building work at the Castle began again under Maria Theresa; then the last general reconstruction took the form of Rococo and Neo–Classical styles (1753–1775).

In 1918 Prague Castle became once again the residence of the head of the newly established Czechoslovak Republic and its first President Thomas Garrigue Masaryk. The entire area was subjected to historical research and excava-

---

Prague
Castle

The gardens
below Prague Castle

tions were begun in the entire grounds. The Castle was renovated and modernized under architect J. Plečnik and his successors. After the second world war investigations were carried out on a large scale in the entire Castle area and continue to this day as does the reconstruction of individual parts of Prague Castle. Since 1 January 1993 the Castle has been the residence of the President of the independent Czech Republic.

A tour of Prague Castle begins at the entrance from Hradčany Square (which can be reached from the Pohořelec tram stop). Another entrance is to be found in U Prašného mostu Street (tram stop, Hradčanská Metro Line A station about 15 minutes' walk away). A third approach is from Klárov (tram stop and Malostranská Metro station on Line A), then up the Old Castle Steps (Staré zámecké schody). The buildings, collections and exhibitions of Prague Castle are open daily from 9–17 hours in summer, from 9–16 hours in winter.

Admission tickets are on sale at the box office in each building or in the Information Centre in the Holy Rood Chapel on the Second Castle Courtyard (open daily 9.00–17.00, in winter to 16.00, closed on Mondays).

The Castle gardens are open to the public daily from 10.00–18.00 in the period April–October. (free of charge). Temporary exhibitions are held by the National Gallery in the **Riding School;** Prague Castle holds short–term exhibitions in the **Imperial Stables,** in the **Theresa Wing,** in the **Royal Summer Palace** and other premises. There is a post office on the Third Courtyard; exchange offices are to be found in the Information Centre and in Vikářská street, where there is also the Castle police. Restrooms (W. C.) are situated

on the Third Courtyard (by the side of St Vitus' Cathedral (in the Royal Palace, in Jiřská street, below the Riding School, at the Royal Summer Palace, in summer in the Garden on the Ramparts (zahrada Na Valech). The Changing of the Guards takes place daily at 12 noon on the First Castle Courtyard. The acccompanying music is played by the Castle Guard band.

The guards on duty at the Castle gateways are changed every full hour. The President's flag on the flagstaff between the roofs of the southern and the westen wing indicates that the President is carrying out his constitutional office on the territory of the Republic. Promenade concerts are held in the Garden on the Ramparts (zahrada Na Valech) at 10.00 a. m. every Saturday from May to October. Concerts of classical music are held in various historical precincts of Prague Castle in the summer months. St George's Basilica (bazilika sv. Jiří), the Ball–Games Court in the Royal Garden (Míčovna v Královské zahradě), the Spanish Hall (Španělský sál) and certain rooms of Lobkowicz Palace (Lobkovický palác) are used as concert halls.

A Tour of Prague Castle

The First Castle Courtyard (První hradní nádvoří) can be reached from Hradčany Square (Hradčanské náměstí) through a Rococo entrance gateway with grille and statues of Battling Giants (I. F. Platzer 1767–1770), present-day copies by Č. Vosmík and A. Procházka, 1901–1902). The courtyard is the result of alterations carried out during the reign of Maria Theresa (1763–1771) to a plan by N. Pacassi. The background to the Court d'Honneur is formed by a wing of the Castle into which the originally free–standing

Matthias Gateway (Matyášova brána, 1614) was incorporated.

It bears the coats–of–arms of the lands ruled by Emperor Matthias, the imperial coat–of–arms and a solemn inscription. In front of the gateway stand two 25 m tall flag–poles erected in 1962. (They were originally designed by J. Plečník as part of the general layout of the courtyard in 1920–1922). Inside the gateway, on the right–hand side, is the Pacassi stairway leading to the state rooms of the President of the Republic. (They are open to the public usually twice a year, in May and in October).

On the left–hand side is Plečnik Hall (1927–1931), which, together with the western wing, was adapted as official anteroom to Spanish Hall (Španělský sál). To the left of the Court d'Honneur is a side entrance to the Castle leading to the **Garden on the Bastion** (zahrada Na baště) with a garden restaurant, laid out by J. Plečnik in 1931.

The Second Castle Courtyard (Druhé

hradní nádvoří) originated in the second half of the 16th century; its present appearance dates from the third quarter of the 18th century (N. Pacassi). The western wing dates from the period of Empress Maria Theresa (1769–75) when it replaced an older building. On the ground floor are remnants of the little Church of St Mary from the end of the 9th century discovered during excavations (not open to the public). The northern wing of the courtyard is taken up by **Spanish Hall** (Španělský sál) with the Rudolph Gallery on the three upper storeys. The inside walls of Spanish Hall (G. M. Filippi, 1602–1606, re–built in the 18th century) were lined with mirrors in 1836, which covered the previous fresco decorations.

The **Rudolph Gallery** (originally Picture Gallery, G. Gargiolli, 1597–1598), together with the adjacent rooms housed the art collections of Rudolph II. The last adaptations of these two halls were carried out in 1866–1868 in anticipation of the coronation of Emperor Franz Joseph I, which then did not take place. At that time the two halls were given unified stucco decorations using older Rococo features. At the present time the two halls are used for official purposes.

Renaissance halls with vaulting are situated on both sides of the gateway leading from Dusty Bridge (Prašný most). They were built by Rudolph II in the 16th cent. as stables for his Spanish horses. The newly adapted halls are used for exhibition purposes: The halls on the right of the gateway form part of the Castle Gallery (not open at present). The area on the left, known as the **Imperial Stables** (Císařská konírna), is used as a separate exhibition hall. The eastern side of the Courtyard is enclosed by the transverse wing

built to a plan by N. Pacassi in 1759–1775. The interior was adapted for state occasions by J. Fragner in 1965. Facing the Matthias Gateway a new entrance to the Office of the President of the Republic was designed by architect B. Šípek (1995).

The southern wing continues along the Third Castle Courtyard to the Royal Palace. The **Holy Rood Chapel** (kaple sv. Kříže) forms the south–eastern corner of the Courtyard. It was built by A. Lurago to a plan by N. Pacassi, 1758–1763, and its present appearance dates from 1852–1856. The high altar has a sculpture by I. F. Platzer and an altarpiece by F. X. Palko. The ceiling frescoes are the work of V. Kandler. This is where the Information Centre is situated.

In the centre of the courtyard stands a Baroque fountain (Francesco de Torre, Jeroným Kohl, 1686); closeby there is a well (14m deep) with a wrought–metal grille (1719). At the present time the first floor areas in all Castle wings are used for official purposes. The second and the third floor of the transverse

The equestrian statute
of St George

wing are occupied by the Office of the President of the Republic.

A passageway through the Transverse Wing leads to he **Third Castle Courtyard** (Třetí hradní nádvoří) with St Vitus' Cathedral as its dominant feature. The courtyard acquired its present form in 1925–1928 (J. Plečnik). Excavations have revealed remnants of the original settlement on this site (a little Romanesque church, remnants of fortifications from the 9th–12th century, foundations of wooden huts, Romanesque and Gothic houses, old roadways. They were covered by a ferro-concrete construction, on which the pavement was placed. Plečnik designed the roofing over older excavations near the cathedral, the layout of the statue of St George and the Eagle Fountain, the Bull Staircase in the southern wing leading to the Garden on the Ramparts.

The **monolith** in the western part of the courtyard was placed there to a plan by J. Plečnik as a memorial to the victims of the first world war. (Height over 16m, made of a single piece of Mrákotín marble). The **equestrian statue of St George** is a Gothic work by George and Martin of Cluj of 1373, partly repaired after 1562. A **post office** has been located in the transverse wing. The northern side of the Courtyard is formed by **St Vitus' Cathedral,** whose western facade with the main entrance faces the passageway from the Second Courtyard. Originally this was the site of a Romanesque rotunda of St Vitus, later replaced by a basilica. (Excavations wtih remnants of the walls can be viewed under the cathedral). The foundation stone to the Gothic cathedral was laid in 1344 in the presence of King John of Luxemburg and his sons. The construction work was supervised by Charles IV. The French architect

Matthias of Arras was in charge of the first building stage (until 1352). Then the work was continued by Peter Parler of Swabian Gmünd (1356–1399) and his sons (until 1406). In that period the oldest, the eastern part was completed; the choir with net vaulting surrounded by a ring of chapels, part of the main tower with the Golden Gate (Zlatá brána), and the foundation stone was laid for the nave and side aisles. The sculptural decorations of the cathedral were made in Parler's masonic lodge from 1360 until the second decade of the 15th century. The Hussite Revolution in the 15th century interrupted building construction, and the eastern part was closed by a provisional wall. The Renaissance helmet and gallery of the tower date from 1560–1562 (B. Wohlmut, H. Tirol). The Baroque onion roof is from 1770 (N. Pacassi). The western part of the cathedral bagan to be built only in 1873 (J. Mocker) and the work was completed by 1929 (K. Hilbert), in time for the thousandth anniversary of the murder of St Wenceslas, the patron

Prague
Castle

The western facade
of St Vitus' Cathedral

saint of the country.

The cathedral is 124 m in length, the transept is 60 m in width, the western facade is 37.5 m wide. The height of the vault in the main nave is 33 m, the towers on the western front are 82 m high, while the main tower rises to 96.6 m. The rose window on the western facade has a diameter of 10.4 m.

The **western facade** is decorated with statues of saints and a relief with portraits of the builders of the cathedral (V. Sucharda, 1929). There are four bronze doors with reliefs by O. Španiel to a design by V. H. Brunner: the central door shows scenes from the building history of the cathedral. On the left door there are scenes from the life of St Adalbert, on the right, the life of St Wenceslas. The stained glass window was designed by F. Kysela. The interior of the cathedral is taken up by the nave with high vaulting leading to the tall choir. Narrower aisles run along the sides of the nave, and they are lined by closely set side chapels. A wreath of choir chapels extends behind the choir. The transept and the nave form an imaginary cross on the ground plan of the cathedral. Inside the cathedral above the pillared arcades runs the **triforium**. The inner side has a gallery of portraits of members of the ruling dynasty of Charles IV, the builders of the cathedral. On the outer side are busts of Christ, the Virgin Mary and the patron saints of Bohemia. In the newer part, to the west, there are busts of persons connected with modern construction work. The **high altar** is Neo–Gothic and dates from 1868–1873 (J. Kranner, J. Mocker). The pews of the canons date from the 17th cent. The large stained glass window with figures was designed by Max Švabinský (1946–48).

The Late Renaissance pulpit dates from the early 17th century. In front of the altar there is the **royal mausoleum** of white marble (A. Collin, 1566–1589). On the upper panel, in high relief, there is the reclining figure of the Emperor and King Ferdinand I, his wife Anna of Jagiello and his son Maximilian II. The side walls are adorned with medallions and busts of the Bohemian kings. The tomb is surrounded by a Renaissance grille. Below it, underground, is the **Royal Tomb** (which can be reached from the Holy Rood side chapel to the right of the mausoleum). In the Crypt are the sarcophagi of Charles IV and his four wives, Václav IV, George of Poděbrady, Ladislav Posthumous, in the background the coffin of Marie Amalie, the daughter of Maria Theresa and the lead coffin of Rudolph II. The Crypt was newly adapted in 1928–1935.

The southern side of the transept formed the dividing line between the old and the new part of the cathedral. It is adorned with the coats–of–arms of the City of Prague (V. Štipl, 1946); the stained glass window was made to a design by M. Švabinský (1937–1939), on the western wall is a memorial to the fallen in the first world war (K. Pokorný, 1921). The northern part of the transept has a **Renaissance organ loft** (B. Wohlmut, 1557–1561). The organ with Rococo ornaments was placed there in 1757.

The first chapel past the transept on the right is the best known chapel in the cathedral. It is consecrated to **St Wenceslas** (Svatováclavská kaple). It was built above the tomb of the Saint in the original St Vitus' Rotunda (Peter Parler, 1362–1367). Facing the entrance is the main altar (renovated by K. Hilbert, 1912–1913). The stone tomb forms one unit with the altar table. The

The interior
of St Vitus' Cathedral

walls of the altar are decorated with slabs of polished semi–precious stones, the walls of the lower part of the tomb bear reliefs by S. Sucharda. The lower strip of the chapel walls is inlaid with more than 1300 pieces of semi–precious stones, the space between is filled with a cycle of mural paintings depicting the Suffering of Christ (c. 1372). The upper part of the walls is covered with scenes from the life of St Wenceslas, made in the workshop of the Master of the Litoměřice Altarpiece (1509). The statue on the eastern side is the work of Peter Parler (1373), the windows onto the Third Castle Courtyard were glazed in 1967 to a design by S. Libenský and J. Brychtová. The inside window is by J. Soukup (1965).

On the western corner there is a door leading to a staircase to the **Crown Chamber** where the Crown Jewels are deposited. Since 1867 this chamber has been closed by seven locks. The Crown Jewels comprise: the Crown, goldsmith's work of the 14th century, based on a Přemyslid crown with the addition of certain older features; a sword from the middle of the 14th century; the scepter and orb from the first half of the 16th century; an 18th century robe and stole. The Crown Jewels are placed on display only on special occasions. **The Royal Oratory** (Královská oratoř) on the right–hand side, next to the Holy Rood Chapel, was built during the reign of Wladislav of Jagiello (1493), whose monogram adorns the crown in the centre of the Oratory; on the bannister are coats–of–arms of the lands under his rule.

In the choir ambulatory there are a **number of chapels** with Gothic tombs of the Bohemian princes and kings, made by the masonic lodge of Peter Parler in the years 1370–1375.

By the pier opposite St Wenceslas Chapel is the **tomb of Count Leopold Šlik** (1723, J. B. Fischer von Erlach, F. M. Kaňka with sculpture by M. B. Braun); a little further on, the silver **tomb of St John of Nepomuk** (1736, J. B. Fischer von Erlach, A. Corradini, J. J. Würth); on the other side, the bronze **statue of Cardinal Schwarzenberg** (J. V. Myslbek, 1891–1895). On the floor of the aisle tomb slabs of Prague bishops. Along the northern wall of the Neo-Gothic part there is an **altar,** the work of F. Bílek (1927) with a wooden relief of the Crucifixion by the same artist (1899).

20th century stained **glass windows** by leading Czech artists add to the artistic wealth of the cathedral. The first window on the right as you enter the building in the St Ludmila Chapel was designed by M. Švabinský; the window in the Chapel of the Tomb of the Lord is by K. Svolinský, that in the Thun Chapel by F. Kysela; in the Hasenburg Chapel the window is the work of C. Bouda. The viewing gallery of the Great Tower can be reached from this chapel, after a climb of 287 steps. The first window to the left of the entrance to the St Agnes Chapel was designed by F. Kysela. There is a bronze statue of St Agnes of Bohemia, made by K. Stádnik in 1989 in the chapel. Karel Svolinský designed the window in the Schwarzenberg Chapel, and the most recent addition to this chapel is a bronze plaque with the Scharzenberg coat–of–arms, placed there in memory of the events in 1989 that led to the fall of the Communist regime in Czechoslovakia. Alfons Mucha designed the window in the New Archbishops' Chapel, where the crypt below the chapel has served as tomb of the Archbishops of Prague since 1909.

In the southern wall of the St Vitus' Cathedral there is a ceremonial entrance from the Third Castle Courtyard to the transept known as the **Golden Gate** (Zlatá brána). It is decorated with a mosaic of the Last Judgment (1370–1371) showing the kneeling Charles IV with his wife Elizabeth of Pomerania. The decorative grille with motives of the zodiac was made by J. Horejc in 1954.

The **main cathedral tower** ends in Pacassi's onion–shaped top. The original Gothic walling rises to the height of 58 m. On the first floor there is a Renaissance bell called Sigismund (1549), weighing 18 tons; on the second floor hang Renaissance bells known as Wenceslas (1542), John the Baptist (1546) and Joseph (1602). The clock with two faces in the upper part of the tower dates from the period of Rudolph II (1597) as does the gilt grille with the letter R.

By the side of the cathedral stands the building of the **Old Provosts' Palace** (Staré proboštství), originally a Romanesque bishops' palace with remnants of Romanesque walls; its present appearance dates from the early 18th century. The southern side of the courtyard is formed by the **Municipal Wing;** its present appearance originated in 1755–1761 when it was rebuilt to a plan by N. Pacassi. In the centre a porch with columns projects into the courtyard. Above it is the Presidents' Balcony, from which the President of the Republic gives a speech on festive occasions.

The eastern side of the Courtyard is taken up by the **Royal Palace** (Královský palác), until the 16th century the seat of the princes and later kings of Bohemia. The central authorities of the state of Bohemia had their offices here until the end of the 18th century, later the palace was used only on isolated occa-

sions. At the entrance stands the **Eagle Fountain** (Orlí kašna – 1664). The Romanesque walls of Soběslav's fortifications survive in the ante–chamber. To the left is the **Green Chamber** (Zelená světnice) where Charles IV presided over minor court sessions, from the early 16th century it was used for court and law sessions. On the ceiling is a fresco of the Court of Solomon transferred here from the court–room of the Burgrave's Palace. Next to it is the **Wladislav Bed–Chamber** (Vladislavova ložnice) with vaulting from the period of Wladislav II of Jagiello, his monogram above the window, and a room that held the Archives of the Land–Rolls. The ante–chamber leads to **Wladislav Hall** (Vladislavský sál) built by B. Ried of Piesting during the reign of Wladislav II of Jagiello (1490–1502). Length: 62 m, width 16 m, height: 13 m. The hall has beautiful twisted rib vaulting and was used for coronation banquets, assemblies of the Estates and for knightly tournaments. Since 1934 the elections of the President of the Republic have taken place here and since 1945 other state assemblies.

In the right–hand corner of the hall a door gives access to the **Ludwig Wing** (Ludvíkovo křídlo) built 1502–1509. These premises hold the rooms of the **Chancellery of Bohemia** (Česká kancelář), the administrative body of the Lands of the Crown of Bohemia. In the absence of the king the governors summoned assemblies here. The two rooms are linked through a Renaissance portal with Ludwig's monogram of 1509. On 23 May 1618 the two hated Governors, Jaroslav Bořita of Martinice and Vilém Slavata of Chlum together with their secretary Fabricius were thrown out of the eastern window in the room at the rear. This act, known as the Defenestration, marked the beginning of the Uprising of the Bohemian Estates and of the Thirty Years' War.

A spiral staircase leads to the **chamber of the Imperial Court Council** (Říšská dvorská rada), which met here during the reign of Rudolph II. It was here that the 27 rebellious squires and burghers were sentenced to death and were executed on 21 June 1621 on the Old Town Square. On the walls are portraits of the Habsburgs, on the left that of King Philip IV of Spain (copy of a picture by Velázquez). Above the tiled stove (17th century) hang two wooden shields which were borne during the funeral processions of Maximilian II and Rudolph II: Between the windows of Wladislav Hall two doors open on to an **observation gallery** and to a terrace, from which there is a lovely view of the gardens below the Castle and the City of Prague.

The eastern wall is decorated with coats–of–arms of Bohemia and Hungary, the date 1500 and the monogram of Wladislav of Jagiello.

Access to the Chapel of All Saints (see U Sv. Jiří Square) can be gained down a staircase and through a portal. On the left–hand side is the entrance to the **Old Diet** (Sněmovna), part of the palace of Charles IV, where the Provincial Court used to assemble. It looks today as it did in the years 1559–1563, when it was renovated by B. Wohlmut. The arrangement of the 19th century furniture gives an idea of the assemblies of the Diet: the royal throne, on the sovereign's right side the chair of the Archbishop, behind him benches for the prelates, along the walls seats for the highest officials, opposite the throne a bench for the representatives of the Estates. By the window on the right there is a gallery for the representatives of the royal towns. Portraits of the Habsburgs adorn the walls.

In the **Hall of the New Land–Rolls** (Místnost Nových zemských desek), to which access is afforded by a staircase, the painted coats–of–arms of the Clerks of the Land–Rolls can be seen. In the room at the rear there is a cabinet of 1562 where the land–rolls were kept. Through a Gothic portal from the time of Charles IV (c. 1355) the **Riders' Staircase** (Jezdecké schody) leads to Wladislav Hall (B. Ried, c. 1500). The staircase has Late Gothic rib vaulting, and its broad steps made it easy for the knights' horses to enter the hall for tournaments. The staircase leads down to an exit to St George's Square, or it is possible to proceed to the **Gothic Royal Palace** and the Hall of the Old Land–Rolls dating back to the time of Přemysl Otakar II. A passage through the neighbouring Gothic arcades leads to a hall with Gothic vaulting dating from the first half of the 14th century and then into Charles Hall. Sessions of the Court of Appeal were held in this hall in the 16th to 18th centuries. Another hall, known as the Old Registration Office, affords access to the **Hall of Columns of Václav IV** (Sloupová síň Václava IV.); it has vaulting from c. 1400. From the palace courtyard it is possible to proceed down into the Romanesque basement of the Royal Palace with remnants of fortifications from the end of the 9th century and parts of the palace of Soběslav and Vladislav.

St George's Square (náměstí U Svatého Jiří) is dominated by the facade of the basilica and the **Convent of St George.** The church was founded by Vratislav I before 921, and it was followed, in 973, by a Convent of Benedictine Nuns, the first such convent in Bohemia. The building underwent numerous alterations, the last in 1657–1680. It was dissolved in 1783 and was used as army barracks. In 1967–1972 the convent premises were adapted as **exhibition halls of the National Gallery in Prague** for its Collections of Bohemian Art from Gothic to Baroque. (Open daily 10 a.m. to 6 p. m. Closed on Monday). The Early Baroque facade of **St George's Basilica** (bazilika sv. Jiří) with a relief of St George and statues of Prince Vratislav and Abbess Mlada, was given its present appearance during purist restoration at the turn of the 19th to 20th century. The colours have recently been renewed. The two eastern towers were added when the church was rebuilt after a fire in 1142. The basilica has been renovated on the basis of excavations in the years 1958–1964 and is now used as concert hall. Inside the nave with 10th to 11th century arcades are the tombs of the Pře-

myslid princes Vratislav I and Boleslav II. Below the double staircase leading to the choir is a crypt from the mid 12th century where the abbesses of the Convent were buried from 1659. The square choir and semi–circular apse have fragments of Romanesque paintings on the vault (c. 1200).

In the adjacent Gothic **Chapel of St Ludmila,** with 14th century adaptations for the relics of this saint brought to the church in 925, there is the marl tomb of St Ludmila, the work of Peter Parler's masonic lodge (c. 1380) and a Neo–Gothic altar dating from 1858. The paintings on the vault are from the end of the 16th century, those on the triumphal arch from the second half of the 15th century. The **Chapel of St John of Nepomuk** along the southern wall of the basilica was added in 1716–1722. It is adorned with an altarpiece and frescoes by V. V. Reiner. The old entrance from Jiřská Street has an Early

Renaissance portal with a relief of St George and the Dragon (now copy). At the south–eastern corner of the square is the portico of the one–time **Institute of Noblewomen** (Ústav šlechtičen) with decorations from 1755. In the 16th century this was Rožmberk Palace. The Institute was set up in the 18th century as a home for impoverished noblewomen. Linked to the Institute is the **All Saint's Chapel** (kaple Všech svatých) with a 1580 portal. The originally Romanesque chapel was last reconstructed at the end of the 16th century when its organ loft was linked up with Wladislav Hall. At that time the earthly remains of St Procopius were brought here from Sázava Abbey, and they are now laid to rest in the Baroque altar on the northern side of the chapel. The high altar is decorated with an altarpiece by V. V. Reiner.

Jiřská Street leads off the southern end of St George's Square. On the right–hand side stands **Lobkowicz Palace** (No. 1), built after 1570 and re-built in the latter half of the 17th century (C. Lurago). Its present appearance stems from 1791. After extensive reconstruction in the years 1973–1987 the permanent **History Exhibition** of the National Museum is housed here, devoted exclusively to our national history. The street ends at a **gateway** from the 13th–16th century leading to the **Old Castle Steps** (Staré zámecké schody) and down to the Malostranská station on Line A of Prague Metro. Outside the gateway on the right is an observation terrace with a view over the historic part of Prague.

Passing through the gateway in the opposite direction up Jiřská Street you will find the **Burgrave's Palace** on the right (No. 4). It has a Baroque gateway adorned with the coats–of–arms of the burgraves. The Renaissance building dates from 1555 (G. Ventura). Inside, the palace and the adjacent buildings are decorated with the works of leading Czechoslovak artists, and cultural programmes and exhibitions are held here. The Toy Museum has a permanent exhibition here (open daily 9.30 a. m.–5.30 p. m.). On one side of the courtyard stands the **Black Tower** (Černá věž), part of the Castle fortification from the first half of the 12th century. Past the palace on the right some steps lead to a view terrace on the right and, on the left to the Dalibor Tower and to the **Golden Lane** (Zlatá ulička), with houses built into the late 16th century Castle fortifications, then about one metre thick. First the Castle sharpshooters dwelt here, later small craftsmen such as goldsmiths, tailors, etc. These houses were repaired in 1952–1955 and now small shops, exhibition rooms and refreshment bars are to be found here. At the end of the little lane stands the **Daliborka Tower** (1436), part of the Castle's Late Gothic fortifications. The tower derives its name from Squire Dalibor of Kozojedy, who was the first to be imprisoned here in 1498. The **White Tower** (Bílá věž) at the other end of the Golden Lane likewise has a dungeon (1584).

From St George's Square along the right side of St Vitus' Cathedral runs **Vikářská Street.** House no. 37, the Chapter Deanery, (Mladota House) has a High Baroque facade dating from 1705. In the house next to it is the renowned Vikárka restaurant. Behind the restaurant is the tower called **Mihulka** or **Powder Tower,** which is open to the public. It was an artillery bastion in the late 15th century and now houses an exhibition devoted to the arts and crafts of the Rudolphinian period and

to the history of the tower itself. From Vikářská Street a passageway will take you to the Second Castle Courtyard. Turning right through the gateway under the northern wing it is possible to reach the **Dusty Bridge** (Prašný most). The northern facade of the gateway itself has a portal by N. Pacassi (1772). The bridge was originally a wooden one. It linked the Castle to the Renaissance garden laid out to the north of the Stag Moat (Jelení příkop). Pacassi replaced the bridge with the present causeway. On the left–hand side of U Prašného mostu Street is the former **Riding School** of Prague Castle (Jízdárna Pražského hradu, No. 3, 5, J. B. Mathey, 1694–1695). It was adapted as art gallery in the late fifties. From the terrace there is a lovely view of the Castle and its grounds. On the right–hand side of the street is the **Lion**

Court (Lví dvůr – no. 6 –). It dates from the end of the 16th cent, and during the reign of Emperor Rudolph II both lions, tigers, lynx and bears were kept there. Opposite the Riding School, on the right side of the street, lies the **Royal Garden** (Královská zahrada). It was laid out from 1534 onwards by Ferdinand I and his successors. The garden is open to the public. Originally it was a Renaissance garden, which was turned into an English park in the early 19th cent. To the right of the entrance is the Presidential Villa and a little further on the building of the Renaissance **Ball–Game Court** (Míčovna), Bonifaz Wohlmut, 1567–69) with rich sgrafitto ornamentation. The statue in front of it represents Night, the work of Matthias Bernard Braun, 1734. Central plaza, about one third along the garden, is adorned by the Hercules Fountain (J. J.

Bendl, 1670). At the eastern end of the garden lies a small Renaissance garden with regular flowerbeds, and in its centre stands the **Singing Fountain** (Zpívající fontána – 1564–68). Its name derives from the sound drops make as they fall on to the bell–metal dish. Behind it rises the beautiful architecture of the **Royal Summer Palace** or Belvedere (Královský letohrádek). There is an entrance to it also from Mariánské hradby street, where there is a tram stop. The Belvedere was built by Italian Renaissance architects in 1538–1564, begun to plans by Paolo della Stella and finished by B. Wohlmut. The Renaissance roof truss has the shape of an inverted ship and is covered with copper plate. The arcades around the building are richly ornamented.

It is now used as exhibition hall. Near the arcade stands the statue of The Genius by Jan Štursa.

The southern gardens at the foot of Prague Castle, the **Paradise Garden** (Rajská zahrada) and the **Garden on the Ramparts** (zahrada Na valech) are now open to the public after extensive reconstruction work. They can be reached in three ways: From Hradčany Square, from the overlook above the Old Castle Steps (Staré zámecké schody) and from the Third Courtyard. The Paradise Garden can be reached from Hradčany Square. It was laid out in the second half of the 16th cent. and adapted by J. Plečnik in 1920–24. Below the monumental staircase stands a large decorative dish made of one piece of Mrakotín marble; along the path a hundred year old yew–tree, the oldest tree in the Castle gardens. By the corner wall is the Matthias pavilion (Matyášův pavilon – 1617) with mural paintings by J. Navrátil.

The Garden on the Ramparts (zahrada Na Valech) begins at the Baroque fountain (1703), its present appearance was likewise designed by J. Plečnik. The path through the garden towards the Old Castle Steps (Staré zámecké schody) affords exceptional views over the City. The garden can be reached from the Third Castle Courtyard down the Bull Staircase (Býčí schodiště). A semicircular look–out with a marl pyramid is to be found where the staircase ends. To the right of this is a viewing pavilion with eight columns. Down the slope below the look–out, in the smaller Hartig Garden (Hartigovská zahrada) is a circular Music Pavilion (Hudební pavilon) built in the 20s of the 18th cent. In the garden are six sandstone sculptures made by Matthias Bernard Braun, which were brought here from the chateau at Štiřín. Two obelisques below the Ludwig Wing of the Castle mark the spot where the Imperial Governors fell furing the Defenestration in 1618. One of the foundation arches of the Theresa Wing (Tereziánské křídlo) serves as entrance to the southern courtyard of the Royal Palace. On the terrace below the Institute of Noblewomen (Ústav šlechtičen) stands Plečnik's largest pavilion, the Bellevue Pavilion, on the wall below it the original torch–bearer angels by Ignaz F. Platzer (c. 1770). Plečnik placed the Hercules Fountain in front of Bellevue Pavilion. The Moravian Bastion (Moravská bašta) has an oval table where President T. G. Masaryk used to sit with his friends. The bastion has as its dominant point an almost 12 m high monolith with an Ionian capital and a gilt globe with stylized thunderbolts. The entrance (or exit) to the Garden on the Ramparts is situated close to the overlook outside the eastern Castle gateway.

The entrance to Prague Castle leads off **Hradčany Square** (Hradčanské náměstí). This Square has kept its ground plan from the Middle Ages when it was the centre of the town of Hradčany. After a major fire in 1541 palaces of the aristocracy and Church dignitaries rose where burghers' houses had stood before.

In the very centre stands a **pest column** with a statue of the Virgin Mary and the figures of the eight patron saints of Bohemia (F. M. Brokoff, 1726). The ornamental candelabrum of the gas lighting dates from the 19th century.

Schwarzenberg Palace (Schwarzenberský palác – No. 2) is an exemplary work of Prague Renaissance palace architecture from the years 1545-1563 (A. Vlach). The facade and the gables are covered with sgrafitto paintings (1567). Inside the palace are pannelled and painted ceilings depicting scenes from Antiquity. The palace houses the Military History Museum. (Open May-October daily 10.00 a.m. - 5.30 p. m. Closed on Monday).

Toscana Palace (Toskánský palác – No. 5) is an Early Baroque building from the years 1689–1691, built to plans by J. B. Mathey. Above the pillared portal are sculptured coats-of-arms of the Counts of Tuscany, who owned the palace from 1718 on. The statues of ancient gods on the attic were made by J. Brokoff.

The statue of St Michael at the corner of Loretánská street dates from c. 1691 (probably made by O. Mosto), below it the Tuscany coat-of-arms (prob. 1720).

Church of St Benedict of the Order of the Bare-Footed Carmelite Nuns, originally the Gothic parish church of the town of Hradčany. The present double-naved church in Baroque style dates from the middle of the 17th cent. It was given to the Carmelite Nuns together with the convent, of which it forms part, in 1792.

Martinic Palace (Martinický palác – No. 8) still has the portal of the original building from the third quarter of the 16th century. After 1620 the palace was enlarged to its present size by Jaroslav Bořita of Martinice, who had it decorated with Renaissance gables and had the Martinice coat-of-arms placed above the portal. During reconstruction work in 1971 sgrafitto decorations with biblical scenes were discovered (second half of 16th and first half of 17th century). The rooms indoors have beamed or painted ceilings. Nowadays the palace is the headquarters of the Commission for the Development of the City of Prague, and exhibitions are held here. **Sternberg Palace** (Šternberský palác – No. 15) was built to plans by G. B. Alliprandi and G. Santini in 1698–1707. The ceilings and walls are adorned with frescoes. The sandstone statues on the staircase come from Clam-Gallas Palace in the Old Town (M. B. Braun). Since 1948 the Palace has housed the permanent exhibitions of the National Gallery. (Open daily 10.00 a. m. - 6 p. m. Closed on Monday).

The Renaissance **Archbishop's Palace** (Arcibiskupský palác, No. 16, middle of 16th century) was given Early Baroque form by J. B. Mathey in 1675-1679. The marble portal and roof structure date from that time. The present Rococo facade, was designed by J. J. Wirch

lead to Hradčany Square linking Hradčany with the Lesser Town (Malá Strana). In this vicinity is the entrance to the Southern Garden (jižní zahrada) of Prague Castle.

The south-western corner of Hradčany Square links up with **Loretánská Street**. When Hradčany was granted a royal charter in 1508 a **town hall** was built (Hradčanská radnice, No. 1, 1601–1604). Its sgrafitto facade with remnants of the imperial coat-of-arms, a picture of Justice and the emblem of Hradčany above the portal date from that time.

Hrzán Palace (Hrzánský palác –No. 9) was originally a Gothic house that belonged to architect Peter Parler; in the 16th century it was re-built in Renaissance style. The embossed portal and parts of the sgrafitto date from that time. The present Late Baroque facade is late 18th century.

The little **Chapel of St Barbara** (Kaplička sv. Barbory), on the right-hand side of the street, stands in the wall of the garden belonging to Trauttmannsdorff Palace and is the work of F. M. Kaňka (1726).

Loretto Square (Loretánské náměstí) is one of the most beautiful in Prague. It dates back to the first quarter of the 18th century.

The left-hand side is taken up by **Černín Palace** (Černinský palác – No. 5), a monumental building of the years 1668–1688, to plans by F. Caratti, adapted by F. M. Kaňka in 1720. It has a Baroque garden. Italian artists contributed to its external and interior decorations. The palace was built for Count Černín of Chudenice, the Imperial Envoy in Venice. After damage caused when the French army occupied Prague in 1742 it was reconstructed to plans by A. Lurago in 1744–1749. The mighty palace

for Archbishop Antonín Přichovský (1746–1765). The front of the building has rich stucco decorations, the Archbishop's coat-of-arms and statues, most of them by I. F. Platzer. Interior decorations from that period include a set of ten gobelins produced in the Paris workshop of the Neilsons (1754–1765) and collections of glass and porcelain. The Archbishopric of Prague is situated here.

The Castle Ramp (Hradní rampa) linking Hradčany Square with Nerudova Street is a much frequented observation point with a lovely view over the historic part of Prague and Petřín Hill framed by modern high-rise buildings in the distance. The ramp was built into the rock in 1638-1644 and was later adapted by G. Santini. A chapel used to stand here, of which only the foundations survive on the present observation area and a staircase that leads to a coffee-house in what remains of the chapel. On the left side of the Ramp with the statue of St Philip Neri (M. J. Brokoff, 1715) the New Castle Steps (Nové Zámecké schody) stairway indoors is adorned with frescoes by V. V. Reiner and sculpture by M. B. Braun. In 1928–1934 the entire palace was re-built to plans by P. Janák, and today it is the Ministry of Foreign Affairs.

On the right-hand side of the Square stands the **Loretto** (No. 77). The heart of this pilgrim centre is the Santa Casa commissioned by Benigna Caterina of Lobkowicz in 1626–1631 and built under the supervision of G. B. Orsi. It is a copy of the alleged home of the Virgin Mary in Nazareth, which, according to legend, was moved to Italy. The decorations on the outside (paintings, figural stucco and reliefs with scenes from the life of the Virgin) were added after 1664. Inside the Santa Casa is a silver altar and a statue of Our Lady of Loretto dating from the third quarter of the 17th century. The courtyard with the Santa Casa has cloisters built by 1664 and later raised by one storey (K. I. Dientzenhofer, after 1740). On the eastern side of the cloister stands the Church of the Nativity (K. I.Dientzenhofer, 1734–1735) with valuable ceiling paintings by V. V. Reiner in the presbytery and by A. Schöpf in the nave. The facade of the Loretto and its tower were designed by K. I. Dientzenhofer in 1720–1722. On the stroke of each hour a clock mechanism sets in motion a carillon of 27 bells in the steeple and chimes the hymn "We greet Thee, Mary, a thousand times". The sculptures on the facade are the work of J. B. Kohl and A. F. Quittainer. The Loretto Treasure is housed on the first floor of the western wing where art treasures, monstrances and other liturgical objects from the 16th to 18th century are on display. The oldest is a Gothic chalice of 1510 and the most famous the Diamond Monstrance of 1698 with six and a half thousand diamonds. The precincts of the Loretto are open daily from 9.00 a. m. – 12.15 and from 1.00 p. m. – 4.30 p. m. Closed on Monday). The northern side of the square is formed by the **Church of Our Angelic Lady** and the **Capuchin monastery** (kostel P. Marie Andělské - No. 6), the oldest Capuchin monastery in Bohemia (1600-1602). Every Christmas a large crib with Baroque figures is installed in the monastery church. To the west of the monastery is a little street known as the **New World** (Nový Svět). It has picturesque little Baroque houses from the 18th and the 19th century and a stylish wine-cellar At the Golden Pear (U zlaté hrušky). The south-western end of Loretto Square opens up to the 14th century suburb of **Pohořelec.** As there were numerous fires in this part the name translates as "scene of fire". The originally Renaissance houses have all been adapted in Baroque style. In the centre of the little square stands a **statue of St John of Nepomuk** (1752) moved here from Hradčany Square.

The corner building, Kučera Palace (No. 22) dates from the second half of the 18th cent., when it was re-built from an originally Renaissance house. The beautiful Rococo facade with rich stucco ornaments dates from that period. Now used by the Komerční banka banking house. On the opposite corner in Keplerova street, close to the tram-stop, stands a statue of the Danish astronomer Tycho Brahe and the German astronomer Johann Kepler (J. Vajc, 1984). In the early 17th cent. they jointly carried out astronomical observations in a building that used to stand where a school is situated today in Parléřova street.

The House At the Šliks (Obecní dvůr

No. 25) belonged to the Counts of Šlik in the 17th cent. After 19th cent. reconstruction it housed a court, orphanage and school.

No. 26 (Broad Court, Široký dvůr) is recorded in the 15th cent. as a road-house with stables. The 1741 Early Baroque portal and gables have survived.

A narrow passageway in the house **At the Golden/Green Tree** (U zlatého/zeleného stromu – No. 8) with the Strahov coat-of-arms above the entrance leads to the **Strahov Courtyard** (Strahovské nádvoří) with the buildings of the Premonstratensian **Strahov Abbey** (Strahovský klášter). The main ap proach is further to the right, up a ramp from Pohořelec, through a Baroque gateway with a statue of St Norbert by J. A. Quittainer. To the left of the gateway is the **Church of St Roch** (kostel sv. Rocha – 1603–1612), the local parish church, a Renaissance buildings with still certain

Gothic features. Nowadays it serves as the Miro Gallery (open daily 10 a. m. – 6 p. m.). In the centre of the forecourt stands a column with a statue of St Norbert (2nd half of 17th century). Behind it is the **Church of the Assumption** (kostel Nanebevzetí P. Marie). Its present Baroque form and the tower date from 1742-1758 (A. Lurago). Originally it was a Romanesque basilica, adapted in Gothic and later Renaissance style with Baroque interior decorations (c. 1750). The high altar has sculptures by I. F. Platzer, the side altars works by J. A. Quittainer During his stay in Prague W. A. Mozart played the organ in this church. To the right of the church entrance stands the Neo-Classical building of the monastery library with the **Philosophical Hall** and the **Theological Hall,** which resulted when a one-time granary was reconstructed by I. J. Palliardi in 1783. The Early

Hradčany

The Theological Hall
of Strahov Abbey

Baroque Theological Hall has a remarkable interior with theological literature in glass-covered cabinets. In the centre of the hall are globes from the first half of the 17th cent. The Philosophical Hall extends over two storeys of the building. The Strahov Library owns more than 130 thousand volumes, including illuminated manuscripts and incunabuli. It is open to the public daily 9.00 a. m. –12.00, 13.00–17.00 Closed New Year, Christmas Day, Easter Sunday.

Behind the church is the entrance into the courtyard of **Strahov Abbey** (Strahovský klášter). It was founded in 1140 by Vladislav II for the Premonstratensian Order. The originally Romanesque building underwent many alterations, the most striking being that in Baroque style in the years 1682–1698 (J. B. Mathey).

The **Museum of National Literature** is to be found in the eastern wing to the left of the courtyard. On the first floor the former abbots' dining hall has been turned into Božena Němcová Hall, where literary evenings are held. On the right-hand side of the courtyard stands the monastery proper around the square Court of Paradise. The entrance vestibule of 1742 – the former Chapter Hall –is decorated with ceiling frescoes by S. Nosecký. In this building is to be found the recently opened **Strahov Picture Gallery** with works from the monasterial collection ranging from Gothic art to Romanticism. The Museum of National Literatura also holds exhibitions

here. Open daily 9.00 – 12.00, 12.30–17.00. Closed on Monday.

The park surrounding the monastery is open to the public. Access is gained from Úvoz Street and an observation path links up with **Petřín Hill** and affords beautiful views over the city. Petřín Hill rises to an elevation of 318 m west of the Lesser Town and its slopes are covered with orchards. The **Church of St Lawrence** (kostel sv. Vavřince) at the top of the hill was originally a Romanesque building, its present Baroque form dates from 1735–1770. **The View-Tower** (rozhledna) is 60 m high and was built for the Jubilee Exhibition in 1891 (F. Prášil) as a copy of the Eiffel Tower in Paris. Open daily April to October, 9.30–22.00. A **labyrinth** (bludiště) from the 1891 Exhibition was later brought here, too. Inside is a labyrinth of mirrors and a diorama showing the battle of Prague students against the Swedes on Charles Bridge in 1648 (K. and I. Liebscher, V. Bartoněk). Open daily April-October, 9.30–17.00

The **Planetarium** (Hvězdárna). was built in 1927–1928. A statue of M. R. Štefánik is situated at the entrance (B. Kafka). The **Hunger Wall** (Hladová zeď) leading from Strahov via Petřín to Újezd was erected on order of Charles IV in 1360–1362 as part of the town fortifications. From the top station of the cable railway from Újezd up Petřín Hill a path leads to Strahov Stadium.

The historic and present-day centre of life in the Lesser Town (Malá Strana), perhaps the most picturesque part of

the Prague towns, is **Lesser Town Square** (Malostranské náměstí). It has retained its characteristic atmosphere with the Church of St Nicholas (chrám sv. Mikuláše) as its dominant feature. The Lesser Town began in the 10th century as a settlement below the prince's castle. The square has always had a lower and an upper part, which received the joint name of Lesser Town Square only in 1869. Most of the oldest buildings were destroyed when the Prague Hussites battled against the garrison at Prague Castle (1415) and later by a big fire in 1541. The town received its present appearance in the 17th and 18th century during, first, Renaissance and, later, Baroque building construction. The square is surrounded by a number of historic houses and palaces with arcades. The premises of some are now occupied by a famous old Prague alehouse, coffee-houses, by wine-cellars Makarská – No. 2, At the Three Golden Stars (U tří zlatých hvězd – No. 8), At the Golden Lion (U zlatého lva), At the Art Patron's (U mecenáše – No. 10). The two parts of the Square are separated by the mighty building of the **Church of St Nicholas** (Chrám sv. Mikuláše) with its main entrance from the upper square. The masterpiece of the leading architects of Prague Baroque, K. Dientzenhofer and his son K. I. Dientzenhofer, arose in the first half of the 18th century, the tower was built by the no less famous architect A. Lurago. The interior decorations of the church are fine examples of High Baroque art. The ceiling frescoes above the nave depict the life of St Nicholas (J. Kracker 1761). Some 1 500 square metres in size, they are among the largest in Europe. The ornamentation of the cupola is the work of F. X. Palko (1751). Below it the four large statues by I. F. Platzer represent the Church Fathers. The gilded statue of St Nicholas above the high altar was made by the same artist.

A number of valuable paintings are by the Baroque master K. Škréta. W. A. Mozart played the organ here during his stay in Prague and nowadays concerts are regularly given in St Nicholas's. The church is open daily from 9.00 to 16.00. Admission fee.

A **Trinity Column** stands in the upper part of the Square, built in 1715 to a design by G. B. Alliprandi as an expression of gratitude that the outbreak of the plague had come to an end. **Lichtenstein Palace** (Lichtenštejnský palác –No. 13) lines the entire western side of the upper square. The originally Renaissance building was reconstructed to its present Neo-Classical form in 1791. In 1620–1627 the palace belonged to Karl von Lichtenstein, who cruelly persecuted the participants of the anti-Habsburg uprising. The building belongs to the Academy of Music, and concerts and exhibitions are held here. (Tuesday-Sunday, 10.00–18.00). The House At the Black Eagle (Dům U Černého orla No. 14) with an apothecary of the same name has Neo-Renaissance sgrafitto.

Smiřice Palace (palác Smiřických – At the Montagues – No. 18) dominates the northern part of the square. In the early 17th century it belonged to the Smiřice family, who had the palace completely re-built. On 22 May 1618 representatives of the anti-Habsburg opposition met here to prepare the Uprising of the Estates against the Emperor and the defenestration of the governors. The palace underwent further reconstruction in 1764–1765. **Sternberg Palace** (Šternberský palác – No. 19) has a Baroque facade from the early 18th century. At the turn of the 18th to 19th century it became a centre of men of culture and science thanks to the efforts of scientist Kaspar

The Lesser Town – Malá Strana

View of the Church of St Nicholas
from Vrtba Garden

Sternberg. In 1770 a Private Society for the Sciences was established here, and it was later re-named the Royal Bohemian Society of the Sciences.

The Late Renaissance Lesser Town Hall (Malostranská radnice – No. 21) is the result of reconstruction work in 1617–1630. From the 15th century until 1784, when the Lesser Town was incorporated into Prague, the Lesser Town Hall was the centre of its political, economic and cultural life. In 1575 the Czech Confession was drawn up here with the aim of legalizing religious freedom and putting forward other demands of the anti-Habsburg opposition of the Estates (see plaque on the building). The building, known as Malostranská Beseda (Lesser Town Club), is used for theatre performances, concerts, exhibitions, etc.

The recently reconstructed **Kaiserstein Palace** (Kaiserštejnský palác – No. 23) came into being when two Gothic houses were linked up. Its present appearance dates from c. 1700. The attic is adorned with allegories of the four seasons. In 1908-1914 the famous opera singer E. Destinová lived here (bust on the palace).

The Jesuit College (No. 25) in the centre of the square was built in 1674–1691. After the dissolution of the Jesuit Order at the end of the 18th century it was reconstructed as administrative building. The neighbouring **Grömling Palace** "At the Stone Table" (Grömlingovský palác/U kamenného stolu – No. 28) originated in 1775 on the site of a number of medieval houses. Mythological statues by I. F. Platzer stand on the attic. The Radetzky Coffee-house was opened here in 1874, later re-named Lesser Town Coffee-House, which serves as such to this day.

Two streets lead off the north-eastern corner of the Lesser Town Square, Letenská and Tomášsská Streets. The latter goes to Wallenstein Square (Valdštejnské náměstí) and Valdštejnská Street. On the left-hand side of **Letenská Street** stands the **Church of St Thomas** (kostel sv. Tomáše), which was built as part of the Augustinian monastery between 1285 and 1379, when the Gothic basilica originated. Repaired in the second half of the 16th and early 17th century and partly adapted in Renaissance style its present appearance dates from 1727–1731, the result of Baroque alterations by K. I. Dientzenhofer. The ceiling paintings in the church are frescoes by V. V. Reiner, the high altar has as altarpiece a copy of a painting by P. P. Rubens (the original is in the National Gallery). The sculptures on the altar (2 large statues) are by J. A. Quittainer and 6 smaller ones by F. M. Brokoff, on the side altars there are several pictures by K. Škréta. The **St Thomas's monastery** (klášter sv. Tomáše – No. 22) was founded as an Augustinian convent in 1285, it was re-built several times, and its present appearance dates from the second half of the 17th century. It serves as old people's home now. The monastery included a brewery (No. 12), founded in 1358, while its present building is of 1763. At the turn of the 19th to 20th century this was the meeting place of leading Czech writers, actors and artists.

The brewery is now a popular ale-house with an open-air restaurant. Adjacent to the ale-house is the wall of **Wallenstein Garden** (Valdštejnská zahrada – see p. 54) which can be reached through an entrance gate in the wall. (Open May-September, daily 9.00 a. m. – 7.00 p. m.).

On the right-hand side of the street is

The Lesser Town – Malá Strana

Vrtba Palace (Vrtbovský palác – No. 5) an outstanding example of High Baroque, dating from 1707-1725, partly designed by G. Santini. The staircase indoors with putti dates from that time, as do those on the attic of the building. In **Tomášská Street,** on the right-hand side, there stands the **House At the Schnells** (U Schnellů – No. 2) with a Neo-Classical facade of 1811. A well-known ale-house is to be found on the ground floor. The **House At the Golden Stag** (U zlatého jelena – No. 4) with a High Baroque facade (K. I. Dientzenhofer. 1725–1726) has a statuary of St Hubert and the Stag by F. M. Brokoff (1726) on the front. The House **At the Kláras** (U Klárů – No. 15) is High Baroque in appearance (1738). The composer V. J. Tomášek lived and died here (memorial plaque) as did graphic artist V. Morstadt. The House **At the**

Three Storks (U tří čápů) is in Empire style with a contemporary house-sign (1820). In it is the stylish Wallenstein inn (Valdštejnská hospoda). **Wallenstein Square** (Valdštejnské náměstí) lies at the end of Tomášská Street. **Ledebour Palace** (Ledeburský palác – No. 3) on the left-hand side was given its present appearance in 1787 when it was rebuilt to plans by I. J. Palliardi. Behind the palace is a terraced garden with a salla terrena. A passageway through the palace leads to an entrance to the gardens below Prague Castle. (open daily 10.00 a. m.–6.00 p. m.). The right-hand side of the square and the ensuing Valdštejnská Street is taken up by the monumental **Wallenstein Palace** (Valdštejnský palác) built for Albrecht of Wallenstein, the Imperial Generalissimo and Count of Frýdlant in 1623–1629. The building was intended

Wallenstein
Garden

to surpass Prague Castle in size and ornamentation. Wallenstein acquired considerable property when land and property was confiscated after the Battle of the White Mountain, 1620, after he had first betrayed many of the Bohemian Estates and then gone over to the service of the Emperor. He won fame as general during the Thirty Years'War, in the end, however, the Emperor took advantage of mutual intrigues and had Wallenstein assassinated in 1634. The construction of the palace was carried out mainly by Italian artists: G. Pierroni, A. Spezza, N. Sebregondi. The main, western front with a Late Renaissance facade and three portals faces Wallenstein Square. Here is to be found the Great Hall with stucco vaulting and a ceiling picture showing Wallenstein as the god of war Mars (B. Bianco, 1630). In the Knights' Hall (Rytířský sál) there is an equestrian portrait of Wallenstein (F. Leuxe, 1631). A chapel in the northern part of the wing rises to the height of the entire palace. It has stucco decorations by B. Bianco and frescoes with scenes from the life of St Wenceslas. The palace was renovated in the early 20th century and again after 1945 when it became the property of the Czechoslovak state. It is used for official and administrative purposes, and concerts are held in the Knights' Hall. In the rear part of the palace there is an exhibition of the Pedagogical Museum of J. A. Komenský (open Tuesday-Sunday, 10.00–12.00, 13.00–17.00).

Wallenstein Garden (Valdštejnská zahrada) is open to the public. The entrance is to be found in Letenská Street. Part of the palace building is a **salla terrena** (G. Pierroni, 1623–1627) with rich stucco ornamentation and pictures (B. Bianco). In the northern part of the salla terrena is a cave with artificial stalagmites and a pool, on the southern side there is a salon with fresco decorations. The bronze fountain in front with a statue of Venus (B. Wurzelbauer, 1599) – now copy – stands at the end of an avenue lined by bronze statues made by Adriaen de Vries. The originals were looted by the Swedes in 1648. The present copies were made in 1913. At the end of the garden is a little lake with a small island on which stands a statue of Hercules, a cast of the original statue by de Vries. Behind the lake the garden is enclosed by the building of the **Wallenstein Riding School** (Valdštejnská jízdárna) of 1630, now used for exhibitions of the National Gallery in Prague. (Open Tuesday-Sunday, 10.00–18.00). The entrance to the building is to be found in the atrium of the Malostranská Metro station at Klárov. **Valdštejnská Street** is lined, on the left-hand side, by a number of **palace buildings:** Pálffy Palace (No. 14), the Small Černín Palace (Malý Černínský palác – No. 12), Kolowrat Palace (No. 10), and Fürstenberg Palace (No. 8), now the Polish Embassy. These palaces, in their Baroque form, are used by various ministries and state authorities. The **palace gardens below Prague Castle,** belonging to the Ledebour, Pálffy, Černín and Fürstenberg palaces, are linked up into one large garden area. Originally they were vineyards and small gardens and were merged when the aristocratic palaces were erected. These gardens flourished in the 18th century when various romantic structures were built with art decorations (salla terrena, garden terraces, loggias, ballustrades, fountains etc.). Entrance see Ledebour Palace p. 53.

Valdštejnská Street leads to Klárov

where the **Malostranská Metro station** on Line A is to be found close to the Wallenstein Riding School. With its unusual layout it is regarded as the most beautiful station of Prague Metro. In the vestibule stands a copy of the statue of Hope by M. B. Braun and two Rococo vases. The garden atrium is adorned with copies of Baroque statues by A. Braun, fountains and a decorative grille.

In the northwestern corner of **Lesser Town Square** (Malostranské náměstí) Sněmovní street leads to the right while Neruda street goes up to Prague Castle. The Lower House of Parliament of the Czech Republic is situated in Thun Palace (No. 4) in Sněmovní street. **Thun Palace** (Thunský palác) was built at the turn of the 17th to 18th cent., and two portals have survived from that time. The present Neo-Classical facade and tympanum with rich relief ornaments of allegorical statues and a Czech lion with the St Wenceslas Crown are the result of reconstruction work around 1800. The Land Diet had its seat here. After the establishment of the Czechoslovak Republic in 1918 the National Assembly took over the building, and on 14 November 1918 the Czechoslovak Republic was proclaimed from this building and the President and the Government were elected here.

One of the loveliest streets in Prague, **Neruda street,** derives its name from the Czech poet and journalist Jan Neruda, who spent his youth here. It was once the main approach route to Prague Castle and is to become part of the renovated Royal Route. Most of the houses have Baroque house fronts, often with characteristic house-signs. **House At the Tom-Cat** (U kocoura – No. 2) has a well-known Plzeň ale-house on the ground floor.

Morzini Palace (Palác Morzinský – No. 5) was designed by G. Santini (1713–1714) and has statues by F. M. Brokoff on the facade. It is now the

Romanian Embassy. **House At the Three Little Fiddles** (U tří housliček – No. 12) was originally Renaissance, its present appearance dates from the 18th century. The house-sign shows that it belonged to the family of the Prague violin-makers, the Edlingers. On the ground floor is a stylish wine-inn. **Valkoun House** (dům Valkounský – No. 14) was re-built by G. Santini who owned it in 1705–1727. **House At the Golden Goblet** (U zlaté číše –No. 16), Renaissance in style, belonged to a goldsmith in c. 1660, hence the house-sign, a golden goblet in an oval cartouche. **House At the St John of Nepomuk** (U sv. Jana Nepomuckého –No. 18) was originally Renaissance and was adapted in Baroque style. It has a house-sign with St John of Nepomuk of 1730. **Thun-Hohenstein Palace** (Thun-Hohenštejnský palác – No. 20) dates from 1721–1726 and was built to plans by G. Santini. The sculptural ornaments are the work of M. B. Braun. Now the Italian Embassy.

The **Monastery of the Theatines** (Klášter theatinů – No. 24) is a Baroque convent building of the late 17th and early 18th century. After the dissolution of the monastery in 1783 it was converted into a dwelling house. The former refectory was used as Kajetan Theatre, where, under the direction of J. K. Tyl, plays were given in the Czech language. **The Church of Our Lady of Unceasing Succour at the Theatines** (Kostel P. Marie ustavičné pomoci u kajetánů) was built for the Order of the Theatines in 1691–1717 in the style of Baroque and Neo-Classical art. The work was completed under G. Santini. The **House At the Golden Key** (U zlatého klíče – No. 27) was originally Renaissance, with Baroque adaptations and the house-sign of a richly decora-

ted key. The **House At Bonaparte** (U Bonaparta – No. 29) dates back to the Gothic period and was given a richly decorated facade in the Baroque period. The **House At the Golden Lion** (U zlatého lva – No. 32), originally Renaissance, has a plaque to show that the Czech art historian and expert on Prague monuments, V. V. Štěch lived and worked here.

The **House At the Golden Horseshoe** (U zlaté podkovy – No. 34) was originally Renaissance in style and belonged to the Italian builder O. Avostalis. It has Baroque adaptations from the 18th century. The house-sign is a picture of St Wenceslas with a real horseshoe on the foot of the horse. On the ground floor is a restaurant **The House At the two Suns** (U dvou sluncŭ – No. 47), Early Baroque style (1673-1693) has the Renaissance portal of the original house. The writer Jan Neruda lived here from 1845 to 1857 (memorial plaque).

Karmelitská Street leads off the southern side of Lesser Town Square in the direction of Újezd. It is lined with aristocratic palaces (Nostitz, Thun, Špork, etc.). **Vrtba Palace** (Vrtbovský palác –No. 25) with its garden, on the right hand side close to the Square, has kept its Late Renaissance form of 1631. A plaque on the front recalls that the Czech painter M. Aleš lived here in 1886–1889. A terraced garden, laid out to a design by F. M. Kaňka in 1720, can be reached through the palace entrance. The statues are the work of M. Braun, the paintings in the salla terrena are by J. Navrátil. At the top of the garden is an observation terrace with a lovely view of Prague Castle and the Lesser Town. The garden is an outstanding example of Baroque garden architecture and sculpture.

The Church of Our Lady Victorious

The Lesser Town – Malá Strana

(kostel Panny Marie Vítězné) on the right-hand side of Karmelitská Street was built by G. M. Filippi in 1611-1613 for the German Lutherans. In 1624 it came into the possesion of the Order of the Carmelites, who altered the church and had a new facade built facing Karmelitská Street, while the original front had looked out over Petřín Hill. On the altar on the right stands the renowned wax figure of the **Prague Child Jesus** (Bambino di Praga). It is of Spanish origin and was presented to the church in 1628 by Polyxena of Lobkowicz. The altarpieces of St Joseph, Joachim and Anna on the right-hand side and St Simon on the left are the work of P. Brandl.

Thun-Hohenstein Palace (Thun-Hohenštejnský palác – No. 18) on the left-hand side of the street has the Baroque appearance of 1747. In the early 19th century it was a hotel where leading personalities were accommodated, among them Admiral Nelson and Lady Hamilton. On the front is a plaque to Dr. M. Tyrš, who lived here from 1841 to 1852.

Karmelitská Street leads to **Újezd.** On the left-hand side is **Michna Palace,** also called Tyrš House (Michnův palác – Tyršův dům – No. 40), originally a Renaissance summer palace of the Kinský family. After the Battle of the White Mountain in 1620 the palace was acquired by Pavel Michna of Vacinov, who had the building reconstructed on a grand scale, and the work was completed by his son Václav Michna to a design by F. Caratti (1640–1650). From 1787 the palace was used as armoury. After 1921 it became the property of the Sokol Physical Education Association, which had it adapted to its present form to plans by F. Krásný. In the courtyard stands a statue of Dr

M. Tyrš, the founder of the Sokol Movement, which has its headquarters here. The Tyrš Museum of Physical Education is open daily 10.00–17.00, closed on Monday.

On the right-hand side of the street is the bottom **station of the cable railway** that goes up Petří Hill from Újezd. It was in operation from 1891–1965 and is again since 1985. The line is 510 m long with one stop halfway by the Nebozizek Restaurant with its observation terrace. The cable railway is in operation daily, 9.25–20.45.

Mostecká Street leads off the southeastern part of the Lesser Town Square towards Charles Bridge. It is lined with little shops selling food, souvenirs and refreshment. The **House By the Wall** (U Hradeb –No. 21), on the right hand side, dates from 1960. In the rear is the U Hradeb cinema and a McDonald's.

The Prague
Child Jesus

Kaunic Palace (Kaunický palác – No. 15) has a beautiful Rococo facade with sculptures by I. F. Platzer. It was built in 1773–1775 on the site of three Renaissance houses. Today it is the Yugoslav Embassy. **House At the Saviour** (U Salvátora – No. 4) on the left-hand side originated in the 19th century when two High Baroque houses were merged. On the facade stands a statue of St Saviour, on the first floor is the relief of a bear, dating from the second half of the 18th century.

The one-time **Customs House** (Celnice – No. 1) is a Renaissance building of 1591 with an original portal and a 19th century facade. The Bridge and Salt Authorities had their headquarters here. On the first floor is a Late Romanesque relief, probably from the mid 13th century. A turn-off from Mostecká Street to the left, just before Charles Bridge, leads to **U lužického semináře Street.** No. 1 is the **House At the Three Ostriches** (U tří pštrosů). In the late 16th century it belonged to a merchant selling ostrich feathers, who had it renovated and adorned with frescoes showing ostrich feathers and with ostriches as house-sign. The painted and beamed ceilings on the first floor date from 1675. In 1714 an Armenian, Deodatus Damayan, opened the first Prague coffee-house in the building. Since reconstruction in 1972–1976 it has been a hotel with a well-kown restaurant on the ground floor. House No. 2, originally Renaissance, was re-built in 1970. Behind it stands a row of houses along the R. **Čertovka,** whose backs are right above the water. This won them the name of Prague Venice. A bridge across the R. Čertovka links U lužického semináře Street with **Kampa Island** (see p. 14).

Lázeňská Street is a turn off Mostecká

Street to the right. The **Church of Our Lady Below the Chain** (kostel P. Marie pod řetězem) was originally a Romanesque basilica with nave and aisles, built in the 12th century, enlarged in the 13th century and adapted in Gothic style in the middle 14th century. The present courtyard between the two towers (1389) and the church proper was the site of a demolished Romanesque basilica. The church was given its present appearance during Baroque reconstruction in 1640–1660 to plans by C. Lurago. The high altar has an altarpiece by K. Škréta, who also painted the picture of St Barbara on the side altar. House No. 4, built by T. Haffenecker 1728-31, houses the Embassy of the Sovereign Order of Maltese Knights.

House At the Baths (V lázních – No. 6) was re-built in Empire style in 1832 and links two buildings. In one of these were the Lesser Town baths already in the 14th century. The house in front was a leading Prague hotel in the 17th to 19th century and had a concert hall. Among outstanding personalities who stayed here is Tsar Peter the Great and the French writer F. R. de Chateaubriand and other famous guests. House No. 11 **At the Golden Unicorn** (U zlatého jednorožce) has a Baroque facade and dates from c. 1740. It used to be a renowned Prague hotel where L. v. Beethoven stayed in 1796.

Lázeňská Street leads to **Maltese Square** (Maltézské náměstí) with a **statue of St John the Baptist** in the centre. It is the work of F. M. Brokoff and was placed there in 1715 in memory of the averted epidemic of the plague. **Nostitz Palace** (Nostický palác – No. 1) of the years 1658–1660 was adapted on several occasions. The decorative oriels, the attic with vases and figures of emperors by M. J. Brokoff are from

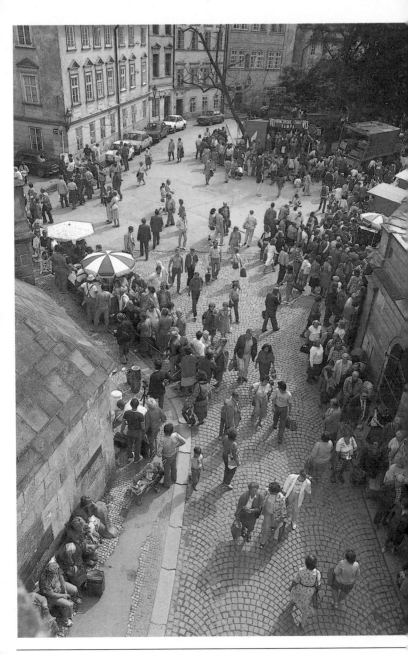

The pottery market
on Kampa Island

c. 1720, the Neo-Classical facade from the late 18th century. The famous Nostitz Picture Gallery was housed in the palace (today in the National Gallery) and a library has survived that bears the name of Dobrovský as indication that outstanding Czech scholars worked for the Nostitz family. Concerts of old music are given in the Empire concert hall on the first floor of the palace (Tuesdays, Fridays, Saturdays at 20.00 hrs). The left wing of the palace is occupied by the Embassy of the Netherlands.

The Japanese Embassy is situated in **Turba Palace** (Turbovský palác – No. 6), a Rococo building of 1767 (J. Jäger). The **House At the Painters'** (U malířů – No. 11) is a Renaissance building of 1531, with Baroque adaptations and more recent renovation in 1931. It has a renowned Prague wine-cellar.

Closeby is **Grand Priory Square** (Velkopřevorské náměstí). The Czech composer J. B. Foerster was born in **Hrzán Palace** (Hrzánský palác – No. 1) in 1859. The palace has a Renaissance portal and gables. No. 2 is the Baroque **Buquoy Palace** (Buquoyský palác), which is the French Embassy today. The Baroque appearance of the **Palace of the Grand Prior of the Order of the Maltese Cross** (Palác maltézského velkopřevora – No. 4) dates from the years 1725-1727 (B. Scotti), It belongs to the Embassy of the Sovereign Order of Maltese Knights. In the vicinity of the palace is the wall of lamentations, poems and utterances associated with the memory of John Lennon.On the banks of the little Čertovka river stands **Grand Priory Mill** (Velkopřevorský mlýn), a Renaissance structure dating back to 1597–98. It was in operation until 1936. The mill-wheel by the little bridge has survived and is again functioning. On the other bank of the Čertovka lies Kampa Island, the most famous in Prague. (see p. 14).

The Lesser Town – Malá Strana

The Old Town Square

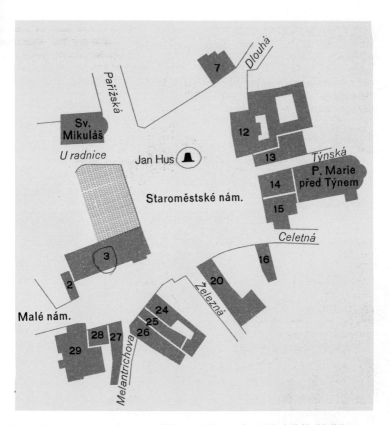

The numbers on the map are in accord with the orientation numbers of the individual buildings given in the text.

THE OLD TOWN – STARÉ MĚSTO

In places where trade routes crossed and an ancient market place existed there gradually grew up the centre of the Old Town – the **Old Town Square** (Staroměstské náměstí). This together with Prague Castle and Charles Bridge is the best known and most frequently visited sight in the capital city. Its largest part is a pedestrian zone and in the summer season visitors have at their disposal little roadside restaurants. Stop for a while in the centre of the Square (best by the Jan Hus Monument, the work of L. Šaloun of 1915) and admire the unique atmosphere, the sensitively restored houses, the busy activities all around. In the centre of the Square you will find the Prague meridian, according

The Old Town – Staré Město

The Old Town Hall

to which time was measured in the Middle Ages. Many events have taken place on the Old Town Square, among them the execution of the leader of the radical Hussite wing, Jan Želivský in 1422. A plaque with his bust hangs on the town hall. George of Poděbrady was elected King of Bohemia here in 1458. In 1621 the leaders of the anti-Habsburg uprising were executed here after the Battle of the White Mountain. The spot is marked by crosses in the pavement in front of the town hall. In 1918 a big demonstration was held here. Another plaque on the town hall recalls the liberation of Prague by the Red Army on 9 May 1945.

The Old Town Hall (Staroměstská radnice – No. 3) has always been the symbol of self-government in the city. It was built when King John of Luxemburg granted the town a royal charter in 1338. An Early Gothic house was adapted as town hall originally, soon the tower was raised and in it a chapel. Before long the premises were too small for the rapidly growing town and so three neighbouring houses, originally belonging to burghers, were joined to it. In 1838–1848 a Neo-Gothic eastern wing was built, which was destroyed by the German fascists during the May uprising in 1945. Only its torso remains. The **Old Town Astronomical Clock** (Orloj) dates back to 1410. It was perfected by Master Hanuš of Růže in c. 1490 and repaired by J. Táborský of Klokotská Hora in 1552–1560. On the hour between 8 a.m. and 8 p.m. the twelve Apostles move past the two little windows of the Clock. The procession begins when Death tolls the bell and ends with the crowing of the cock. The Astronomical Clock includes a little statue of a Turk and allegories of avarice and vanity. The circular sphere below the windows represents the medieval perception of the universe. It measures time and shows the movements of the Moon and the Sun around the Earth. The lowest part is a calendar with paintings by J. Mánes of 1865. The twelve inner medallions show the zodiac, the twelve outer ones have motives from the life of the rural people. This is a copy of the original, which is to be found in the Museum of the City of Prague.

The richly decorated portal of the main entrance to the Town Hall with figural and plant motives and the neighbouring window with the coats-of-arms of Bohemia and the Old Town date from the Late Gothic reconstruction with the participation of M. Rejsek. Another point of interest on the articulated facade of the Town Hall is the Early Renaissance window from after 1520 with the coat-of-arms of the Old Town and the incription Praga caput regni. The Gothic oriel window of the chapel was built before 1381, on the outside it is decorated with emblems from the late 15th cent. Part of the interior of the Town Hall is open to the public. The Gothic vaulting of the vestibule is covered with mosaics, made to cartons by M. Aleš in 1936–1939. The ancient halls on the ground floor are used for exhibitions. A large assembly hall was furnished for official purposes in 1879-1880; it is decorated with large canvases by V. Brožík. The Old Council Chamber still retains its early 15th century form. The Wedding Hall of the Old Town Hall is the most in demand in Prague throughout the year.

A unique view of the Old Town and the historic core of Prague can be gained from the gallery of the Tower (total height 69.5 m.). One gets a clear picture of the irregular network of the

streets in the Old Town and the straight lines of the roadways in the New Town, which was laid out in a modern manner already in the 14th cent. The Town Hall is open to the public. Tours are organized by the Prague Information Service. A Prague Tourist Information Office is located in the building.

Týn Church (kostel P. Marie před Týnem) with its two characteristic 70 m tall steeples is the dominating feature of the Old Town Square. It stands on the site of older churches; its construction began in the middle of the 14th cent. and lasted until 1511. Further repairs were made after a fire in 1679. Predecessors of Master Jan Hus, J. Milič of Kroměříž and K. Waldhauser, gave sermons here, and later this was the main church of Hussite Prague under the Hussite Archbishop J. Roky-

---

The Old Town – Staré Město   St Nicholas' Church

The Old Town Square,
a bird's eye view

cana. The church reverted to the Catholic Church again in 1621. It has a mighty nave and aisles. Above the high altar and the side altars are altarpieces by famous painters, K. Škréta, A. Stevens, J. J. Heinsch, J. Hellich. The church has a Gothic Madonna Enthroned, a stone baldaquin by M. Rejsek of 1493, a valuable Gothic sedile, a relief by F. M. Brokoff, a pewter baptismal fond and a pulpit dating from the 15th cent. Closeby is the marble tomb of the Danish astronomer Tycho de Brahe (1601).

The entrance to Týn Church is located in the arcades of the old Latin School. There is a small gallery, and tickets can be purchased there for concerts, which are held almost daily during the main tourist season.

The Church of St Nicholas (Kostel sv. Mikuláše) contrasts with the Gothic Týn Church by its Baroque shape. Its present appearance dates from 1732-1735, to plans by K. I. Dientzenhofer. The southern front with the main portal is adorned with statues by A. Braun, the frescoes in the dome and side chapels are the work of P. Asam. Concerts are given in the church. Close to the church, at the end of Pařížská Street, is a small fountain with dolphins (1905). The church is now used by the Czech Hussite Church. – On the adjacent house (U radnice Street, No. 5) there is a plaque with a bust of the writer Franz Kafka, who was born here in 1883.

Goltz-Kinský Palace (No. 12) is a Late Baroque building, erected by A. Lurago in 1755–1765. It now houses the Graphic Collections of the National Gallery and termpoary exhibitions are held there. The Old Town Square is surrounded by impressive **burghers' houses** with Gothic, Renaissance, Baroque and Rococo facades. In the basements survive parts of the one-time Romanesque houses (the level of the Old Town Square was gradually raised several metres). Next to Goltz-Kinský Palace stands the most valuable of the houses in the Old Town, known as **At the Stone Bell** (U kamenného zvonu – No. 13). It was re-built in the second quarter of the 14th cent. as a town palace, probably for King John of Luxemburg. The architecture is unique east of the Rhine. The house-sign was built into one corner. Today the premises are used for exhibitions and concerts are held in the upstairs hall. (Open daily 10 a. m.-6.p.m. Closed on Monday). The two characteristic buildings in front of Týn Church with Gothic arcades and rib vaulting belong to Týn School (No. 14, originally a Gothic house with two gables in the style of the Venetian Renaissance, on the ground floor a stylish coffee-house U Týna; the other house is known as At the White Unicorn).

The **southern side** of the Old Town Square is the longest and it has these sights: Štorch House – No. 16, with paintings on the facade made to designs by M. Aleš – St Wenceslas; House At the Stone Ram (U kamenného beránka – No. 17, Renaissance facade); House At the Stone Table (U kamenného stolu – No. 18); an Old Town restaurant with tables outside (No. 19, remains of Romanesque vaulting); House At the Golden Unicorn (U zlatého jednorožce – No. 20, Baroque facade, Gothic portal, passageway with net vaulting, where B. Smetana opened a music school in 1848). In the block between Železná and Melantrichova Street there are to be found: an Early Baroque house with a Madonna and Child (No. 24), House At the Blue Star (U modré hvězdy – No. 25). Beyond Melantrichova Street there is House At the Ox (U vola –

The Old Town – Staré Město

No. 27), the monastery of the Servites (No. 28, Renaissance portal), House At the Golden Angel (U zlatého anděla – No. 29, with a corner statue of St Florian and the U princů restaurant with tables in the open). In close vicinity of the town hall stands a richly decorated Renaissance house with sgrafitto known as House At the Minute (U minuty – No. 2). Of the original mediaeval buildings on the northern side of the Old Town Square only the former Baroque monastery of the Paulines survives (No. 7), the rests was demolished during slum clearance work at the end of the 19th cent. On their site now stands the building of the Ministry of Economic Affairs (No. 5 and 6, with shops selling souvenirs, bijoutery and glass and Café Tschibo on the ground floor). **The Little Square** (Malé náměstí) is immediately adjacent to the Old Town Square. Its triangular shape recalls the directions of trade routes in the early Middle Ages. In the basements of the existing houses can be seen remnants of Romanesque and Early Gothic build-

ings. In the centre a fountain with a wrought iron grille (1560). The Neo-Renaissance three-storey Rott House (Rottův dům – No. 3) dates from 1892 and is covered with murals to cartons by M. Aleš. Richter House (Richterův dům, No. 11,) has a passageway leading to Michalská Street. House No. 12 At the Golden Lily (U zlaté lilie) has a fine house-sign and a small gallery inside. An old Prague pharmacy with old furnishings exists in the House At the Golden Crown (U zlaté koruny – No. 13).

Behind Týn church is an enclosed area known as **Ungelt** or also Týn. This fortified courtyard with two gateways was the centre of international trade with a customs house from the 11th cent. The original character was altered during reconstruction in the 16th cent., the most valuable Renaissance burgher's house from that time is Granovský House with a loggia on the first floor and remains of the original Romanesque building in the basement. Extensive reconstruction is under way at present; the buildings are to be adapted for cultural purposes and the needs of tourism.

Opposite the eastern entrance to Ungelt, in Malá Štupartská Street, there stands one of the most outstanding Baroque churches in Prague **St James's** (kostel sv. Jakuba). An original church existed here in c. 1232 as part of the Minorite monastery (Gothic cloisters of this survive). The grandiose Gothic reconstruction in the 14th cent. imprinted its character on the present-day Baroque appearance of the building (1609–1702). The nave and aisles are decorated with frescoes by F. Voget (1736), the altarpiece on the high altar is the work of V. V. Reiner (1739), several other canvases are by P. Brandl.

A plaque to honour
Franz Kafka

67

An imposing Baroque tomb of J. V. Vratislav of Mitrovice from the early 18th cent. with statues by F. M. Brokoff was designed by J. B. Fischer von Erlach. The church has excellent acoustics and is regularly used for concerts.
Celetná Street links the Old Town Square with the Powder Tower and Na Příkopě Street. It is a pedestrian zone and has recently been restored as the first section of the Royal Route. It is a popular place for promenades and shopping expeditions, A number of wine-cellars, restaurants, snack-bars, exchange offices and shops are found in this street and the newly restored passageways. The most interesting buildings: Sixta House (Sixtův dům, No. 2, Baroque with a Romanesque core), Hrzán Palace (Hrzánský palác, No. 12, Baroque with surviving Romanesque vaulting in the basement), Caretto-Millesimi Palace (Caretto-Millesimovský palác) No. 13, Baroque, 1756, to plans by A. Lurago with walls of the Gothic house), Menhart House (Menhartův dům – No. 17), attractive courtyard with a Baroque statue of a woman in the centre, in the entrance a statue of Hercules with the Lion, with a stylish wine cellar At the Spider (U pavouka), Buqouy Palace (Buquoyský palác – No. 20), since 1773 property of Charles University, House At the Black Mother of God (U černé Matky Boží – No. 34), fine example of Cubist architecture, built 1911–1912 to plans by J. Gočár, at the corner a 17th cent. sculpture of the Virgin Mary), Here is the **Museum of Czech Art,** open daily 10.00-12 noon, 1 p. m.-6 p. m. closed on Monday). The Mint (mincovna) – No. 36, in the 14th cent. the Court of the Queens of Bohemia linked with the King's Court on the site of the present Municipal House (Obecní dům), from the 15th

cent. until 1783 used as Mint, the present building dates from 1755, statues of miners by I. F. Platzer.
The Powder Tower (Prašná brána) forms the end of Celetná Street and is a monumental gateway to the Old Town. There was a gate here already in the first half of the 13th cent., but after the foundation of the New Town it lost its strategic importance. In 1475 King Vladislav I began to build a representative New Gate (Václav of Žlutice, from 1478 Matěj Rejsek of Prostějov) in close vicinity of his residence, the Royal Court. In 1485 the King moved to the Castle, building construction came to a stop and the unfinished gate was used throughout the 17th and 18th cent. as store for gunpowder (hence its present name). It was given its present form during Purist reconstruction by J. Mocker in 1875–1886. Gothic and Neo-Gothic sculptural decorations: on the first floor statues of Přemysl Otakar II and Charles IV (eastern side) and George of Poděbrady and Wladislav II (western side). The tower is 65 m high, the gallery is open to the public.

The area between Fruit (Ovocný) and Coal (Uhelný) Market (trh), Havelská Street and Rytířská Street was settled under King Václav in connection with the foundation of **St Gall's Town** (Havelské Město) in c. 1235. This part of the Old Town lies between the Old Town Square and the border of the New Town; it is a busy area where shopping and catering establishments are now being opened. The narrow **Melantrich Street** (Melantrichova) begins opposite the Old Town Hall and is the shortest link between the Old Town Square, Na můstku Street and Wenceslas Square. – Parallel to it runs **Železná street** ("Iron Street"), part of the

pedestrian zone. On the left side, at the corner of Ovocný trh (Fruit Market) begins the extensive building complex of the **Carolinum** – the seat of Charles University, the oldest university in Central Europe, founded by Emperor Charles IV in 1348. During the reign of Václav IV the university acquired these premises, which have gradually been enlarged. – On the first floor of the Carolinum is the Great Hall, used for graduation ceremonies and solemn occasions. It is adorned with a statue of Charles IV in bronze and a large gobelin depicting Charles IV in front of St. Wenceslas. Adjacent to the Hall is the Chapel of SS Cosmas and Damian with a richly decorated oriel and gargoyle (in the direction of the Theatre of the Estates). The Carolinum was given its Baroque form during reconstruction in 1718 to plans by F. M. Kaňka. The modern main entrance to the Rector's Office of Charles University leads off the Fruit Market where a fountain with statues of lions plays in the forecourt.
Next to the Carolinum stands the Neo-Classical building of the **Theatre of the Estates** (Stavovské divadlo) built in 1781–1783 by Count F. A. Nostitz-Rhieneck. The first Czech performance was

given in 1785. Mozart's opera Don Giovanni had its first ever performance here. From 1799 the theatre belonged to the Bohemian Estates. In 1834 a play by J. K. Tyl was performed here which included what was to become the Czech national anthem.
Havelská Street links Železná and Melantrichova Streets with the Coal Market. The **Church of St Gall** (kostel sv. Havla) has always been an important one in the Old Town. Its Baroque form dates from the end of the 17th cent., the facade of 1722–1729 was probably built to plans by G. Santini, and despite Baroque adaptations the original Gothic interior with rib vaulting survives. In the side chapel on the right is the tomb of painter K. Škréta. – Part of the street is a flower and vegetable market. Arcades have survived in the houses along the northern side. On the southern side the corner house has been renovated and a children's bookshop opened. – The narrow street running parallel, **V kotcích Street,** has long been the centre of trading. This lane used to run down the centre of a covered market-place. The old tradition continues in little shops and stalls selling texiles.
In **Rytířská Street** ("Knights' Street") there used to be a Carmelite monastery – No. 31, used for years now as Centre of Russian Culture with a shop and restaurant. It houses the Black Theatre and an art gallery. Next to it stands the Neo-Renaissance building of the Savings Bank (1892–1894). Inside is a small exhibition hall and a richly decorated hall with bank counters on the first floor. The House At the Blue Column (U modrého sloupu – No. 16) – at the corner of Na můstku dates from the time when St Gall's Town was built. It stood by the walls of the Old

The Estates
Theatre

Town and was used for dwelling and defence as shown by the tall tower of sandstone (now with a Baroque front) and the small Gothic window in the rear of the house.

Rytířská Street ends at the **Coal Market** (Uhelný trh), where the Neo-Classical fountain in the centre (1797) has vine motives. W. A. Mozart used to stay in the House At the Three Golden Geese (U tří zlatých hus – No. 1). On the little square is a well-known ale-house At the Two Cats (U dvou koček), and at the beginning of Michalská Street there is a wine-cellar and a shop selling South Moravian wines.

Close to the Coal Market, in Martinská Street, is one of the oldest churches in Prague **St Martin's-in-the-Wall** (Kostel Sv. Martina ve zdi). The original building was Romanesque dating from 1178–1187, and all around it was the settlement of Újezd sv. Martina. Part of it was later incorporated into the Old Town and the southern wall of the church became part of the town fortifications. The present church is the result of Late Gothic reconstruction; it is used by the Evangelist Church of the Czech Brethren. In 1414 the sacrament was first given to the altar laymen in this church in the Utraquist manner i.e. bread and wine from a chalice. A plaque on the outer wall shows that this is the burial place of members of the family of sculptors, the Brokoffs.

Karlova Street, a further section of the Royal Route, begins at the Little Square. It has several sharp corners and leads to the Square of the Knights of the Cross (Křižovnické náměstí) by Charles Bridge. On both sides stand medieval houses with Romanesque and Early Gothic basements and more recent Renaissance and Baroque facades.

Outstanding among these are: House At the Golden Well (U zlaté studně – No. 3) with a rich Baroque facade and an oriel, with a wine cellar in the basement. House At the Golden Serpent (U zlatého hada – No. 20) with a coffee-house of the same name. In 1714 the Armenian Damayan lived here; he was the first to sell coffee in Prague streets. Unitaria Palace – (No. 8, facade probably by G. Santini) with a Theatre, House At the Green Tree (U zeleného stromu) – No. 4, where the astronomer J. Kepler lived 1607–1612), and finally Colloredo-Mansfeld Palace (No. 2) from before 1735. An interesting place to stop is the shop (No. 12), which sells objects of folk art and handicrafts, and the ancient ale-house At the Fine Jug (U malvaze) No. 10.

Husova Street has many places of interest. It crosses Karlova Street at the Clam-Gallas Palace (No. 20), a mighty Baroque building erected to plans by J. B. Fischer von Erlach in 1715–1730 with sculpture by M. B. Braun (four Titans on both portals) with valuable frescoes by C. Carlone. The building now houses the Archives of the City of Prague. The building of the Bohemian Museum of Art (No. 19) dates from the second half of the 16th cent. Romanesque halls survive in the basement. – In its vicinity stands the popular Plzeň ale-house At the Golden Tiger (U zlatého tygra – No. 17). House No. 15 has a fine house-sign with vine motives. – A short turn into Řetězová Street leads to the **House of the Squires of Kunštát and Poděbrady** (No. 3). This residential Romanesque palace from the second half of the 12th cent. is the best that has survived in Prague (Romanesque vaulting, columns, portal etc.). In 1444–1453 it was the house of the Governor of Bohemia, George of Po-

---

The Old Town – Staré Město

the German reformer T. Müntzer spoke here. After the Thirty Years' War the chapel became the property of the Jesuits, and when the Order was dissolved in 1786 the building was demolished. It was re-built to its original form by J. Fragner in the early fifties of this century. The only parts that survive of the Gothic structure are some of the window jambs, parts of the outer walls with mural paintings based on medieval chronicles (e. g. the Jena Codex). Next to the chapel the preacher's house has also been renewed; it was here that Jan Hus lived and wrote his works. Likewise re-built is the neighbouring Nazareth College with the J. Fragner Exhibition Hall. – An extensive complex of buildings on the western side of Bethlehem Square belongs to the **House U Halánků** (No. 1). In the 19th cent. it was the property of the Bohemian industrialist and patron of culture, and also the founder of the Club of Czech Tourists, Vojta Náprstek. In 1862 he founded a museum here and its collections were enlarged by gifts from Czech travellers so that he had a new museum building erected at the rear in 1886. Today this is the **Náprstek Museum of Asian, African and American Cultures.** (Open daily 9 a. m.–12 noon, 12.45–5.30 p. m. Closed on Monday). The large complex of buildings of the **Clementinum** covers the space between the Square of the Knights of the Cross, Karlova Street and Mariánské Square (with the building of the **New Town Hall** of 1908–1912, where the City Council has its offices, and the Municipal Library). The Clementinum covers an area of 2 ha and is the largest building of the historic core after Prague Castle. Originally here stood 25 Old Town houses, several churches and gardens and a monastery. The Order of

děbrady, who later became king and had the entire palace built. The building is open to the public in summer (May-September 10 a. m.–6 p. m.) and exhibitions are held here. – The only ecclesiastical building in Husova Street is the Gothic **Church of St Giles** (kostel sv. Jiljí), with two towers, built 1339-1371 by bishop John of Dražice and the first Archibishop of Prague Arnošt of Pardubice (their coats-of-arms are on the front). The interior is Baroque, the frescoes by V. V. Reiner date from 1733-1734; he also painted the picture of St Wenceslas and was buried in the left-hand aisle. – House No. 5 belongs to the Czech University of Technology; in 1707 the first Bohemian school of engineering was set up here. Husova ends at a crossroad of several narrow Old Town streets. On the right is **Bethlehem Square** (Betlémské náměstí). It is dominated by the **Gothic Bethlehem Chapel** of 1391–1394, where Master Jan Hus preached his sermons 1402–1413. Up to 3 000 persons could be present. Other Hussite preachers were working in the chapel, too, and in 1521

Bethlehem
Chapel

the Jesuits acquired the land on arrival in Prague from the Dominican monastery with the Church of St Clement, and gradually bought up the neighbouring houses to enlarge the Clementinum. They set up a school, a printing press, a theatre and from 1622 Charles University came under them. – The original **Church of St Clement** was replaced by a Baroque building in 1711–1715 to plans by K. I. Dientzenhofer, with sculptural ornaments by M. B. Braun, and an altarpiece of St Linhart by P. Brandl. The church now belongs to the Greek-Catholic Church; the entrance is on Karlova Street. – On Knights of the Cross Square (Křížovnické náměstí) is the entrance to the **Church of St Saviour** (kostel sv. Salvátora), a Renaissance building completed in 1601, with Baroque additions, the towers date from 1714. Interior decorations by J. J. Bendl, J. Hering, K. Kovář. – The tallest **tower of the Clementinum** is an astronomical and meteorological observatory. – The largest building is the former **Jesuit College** dating from 1653–1726. The largest hall is the summer refectory, now a study-room, and the most valuable is the Library Hall on the first floor with frescoes symbolizing science and the arts.

On the third courtyard is the entrance to the **Chapel of Mirrors** (Zrcadlová kaple) built by F. K. Kaňka in 1724. It has rich stucco decorations with mirrors and is used for exhibitions and concerts. On the first courtyard stands a statue of a Prague Student, in memory of the defence of Prague against the Swedes in 1648. – The Clementinum is now used by the National Library, which owns more than 5.5 milion volumes, valuable manuscripts, among them the Vyšehrad Codex of 1085, and by the Technical Library. The buildings

on the **Square of the Knights of the Cross** (Křížovnické náměstí) form a fine architectonic unit. From there is a unique view of the R. Vltava, the Lesser Town and Prague Castle. The square has on one side the facade of the Church of St Saviour, while the northern side is taken up by the **Church of St Francis** (Kostel sv. Františka) with the Monastery of the Knights of the Cross with the Red Star. The Baroque building with a unique dome dates from 1679–1689 (to plans by J. B. Mathey), inside in the right-hand side chapel stands a Late Gothic statue of the Virgin (1483), the dome is painted with frescoes by V. V. Reiner, showing the Last Judgment (1722), altarpieces by J. K. Liška and M. Willmann. – At the corner a vine column with a statue of St Wenceslas (J. J. Bendl, 1676), around it remnants of the pavement of the original Judith Bridge. – The Neo-Gothic **statue of Charles IV** was erected in 1848 on the occasion of the 500th anniversary of the foundation of the university (allegories of university faculties).

The Old Town Bridge Tower (Staroměstská mostecká věž) stands on the first pillar of Charles Bridge. It is the work of P. Parler and was completed before 1380. On the Old Town side it has rich sculptural decorations (coats-of-arms of the lands of the Crown of Bohemia at the time of the reign of Charles IV, statues of St Vitus, the patron of the bridge, Emperor Charles IV and his son Václav IV, above them the country's patron saints St Adalbert and St Sigismund). The Gothic paintings in the gateway were renewed in 1877. In the years 1621–1631 the heads of 10 Bohemian squires were exhibited on the tower as a warning following their beheading after the Battle of the White

Mountain. The gateway was the scene of battles in defence of Prague against the Swedes in 1648 and the revolutionary Whitsuntide events in 1848. The tower is open to the public daily 10 a.m. –6 p. m.

Not far from the tower are several buildings associated with work on the river: the water tower, the former mill, a weir, a dam stretching from the building of the Smetana Museum to Charles Bridge, and public baths. Restaurants, a theatre, sale of souvenirs and an exchange office are located here. The Smetana Museum can be reached along **Novotný's Footpath** (Novotného lávka). From the Smetana Monument in front there is the best view of the Hradčany panorama and the Smetana Embankment as far as the National Theatre.

A quite unique sight and a place for promenades, meeting people and ever new views of both banks of the Vltava

Charles
Bridge

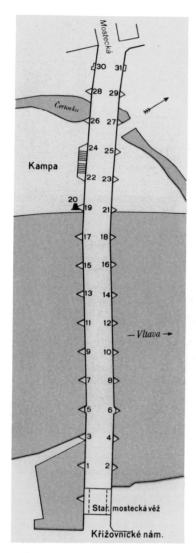

1 St Ivo (M. B. Braun, 1711)
2 The Madonna with the kneeling St Bernard (M. W. Jäckel, 1709)
3 SS Barbara, Margaret and Elizabeth (F. M. Brokoff, 1707)
4 The Madonna, SS Dominic and Thomas Aquinus (M. V. Jäckel, 1708)
5 The Pietá (E. Max, 1859)
6 The Calvary (the gilded bronze corpus was cast by H. Hilger in 1629, the stone statues are by E. Max, 1861)
7 St Joseph with the Child (J. Max, 1854)
8 St Anne (M. V. Jäckel, 1707)
9 St Francis Xavier (F. M. Brokoff, 1711)
10 SS Cyril and Methodius (K. Dvořák, 1928-1938)
11 St Christopher (E. Max, 1857)
12 St John the Baptist (J. Max, 1857)
13 St Francis Borgia (F. M. Brokoff, 1710)
14 SS Norbert, Wenceslas and Sigismund (J. Max, 1853)
15 SS Ludmila and Wenceslas (M. B. Braun, 1730)
16 St John of Nepomuk (the oldest statue on Charles Bridge, 1683, cast by the Nuremberg bell-maker J. W. Herold to a design by M. Rauchmüller and a model by J. Brokoff)
17 St Francis (E. Max, 1855)
18 St Antony of Padua (J. O. Mayer, 1707)
19 St Vincent of Ferrari and St Procopius (F. M. Brokoff, 1712)
20 Roland (L. Šimek, 1884, on the bridge pillar where an early 16th century statue stood before)
21 St Jude Thaddaeus (J. O. Mayer. 1708)
22 St Nicholas of Tolentino (J. B. Kohl, 1708)
23 St Augustine (J. B. Kohl, 1708)
24 St Luitgard (M. B. Braun, 1710), artistically the most valuable statue on the bridge
25 St Cajetan (F. M. Brokoff, 1709
26 St Adalbert (J. M. Brokoff, 1709)
27 St Philip Benitius (M. B. Mandl, 1714)
28 SS John of Matha, Felix of Valois and Yves with the figure of a Turk guarding imprisoned Christians (F. M. Brokoff, 1714)
29 St Vitus (F. M. Brokoff, 1714)
30 St Wenceslas (J. K. Böhm, 1858)
31 St Saviour and SS Cosmas and Damian (J. O. Mayer, 1709

The Old Town – Staré Město

is **Charles Bridge** (Karlův most). In the tourist season it is the venue of painters and musicians where souvenirs are for sale, and tourists of the whole world meet. Charles Bridge had its predecessor in the early Middle Ages when a wooden bridge stood slightly further downstream. In 1158–1160 this was replaced by the stone-built Judith Bridge which, in turn, was destroyed by floodwater in 1342. The construction of Charles Bridge started in 1357 under the supervision of P. Parler, and it was completed in the early 15th cent. The bridge is 520 m long, 10 m wide and rests on 16 pillars. The building material is sandstone. From the 17th cent. on it gradually became a unique gallery of statues under the open sky (30 groups of statues, by stages replaced with copies). In 1393, on order of King Václav IV, the vicar general John of Pomuk was drowned under Charles Bridge. In 1729 he was sanctified as St John of Nepomuk.

The counterpart to the Old Town Bridge Tower are the **Lesser Town Bridge Towers** (Malostranské mostecké věže).

The lower tower, which tends to disappear when viewing the higher one, was part of the fortifications of the left bank settlement already in the 12th cent. It was adapted in Renaissance style at the end of the 16th cent. The taller of the two towers was built in the middle of the 15th cent. and is open to the public. The observation gallery is open daily 10 a. m.–6 p.m. On the gateway that links the two towers are the coats-of-arms of the lands under King Václav IV.

Certain parts of the Old Town and Josefov were cleared at the turn of this century. **Kaprova Street** dates from that time. Here is to be found Staroměstská Metro station of Line A (at a depth of 28 m). The street ends in **Jan Palach Square** (Náměstí Jana Palacha) with several monumental buildings: The Rudolfinum, a Neo-Renaissance building of 1876-1884 built to plans by J. Zítek and J. Schulz, with the Dvořák Concert Hall and exhibition halls, the Faculty of Arts of Charles University (1924–1930), the School of Decorative Arts (a Neo-Renaissance building, 1885). Close to

Detail of the Crucifixion
on Charles Bridge

The interior
of Saint Agnes Convent

the square in 17. listopadu Street is the Museum of Decorative Arts (Uměleckoprůmyslové museum), a Neo-Renaissance building of 1897–1901. Underground parking below the park. A. J. Mánes statue stands close to the, Rudolfinum, in the park on the embankment. From there new views open up to the Lesser Town and Hradčany. – **Pařížská Street** links the Old Town Square with Curie Square (Náměstí Curieových) with the Faculty of Law of Charles University and the Inter-Continental Hotel. The street is lined with airline and travel agencies. The houses on both sides are tall apartment blocks in Art Nouveau and Neo-Baroque styles. The grounds of **St Agnes Convent** lie in the northern part of the Old Town along Na Františku Embankment. The convent was founded in 1233 by King Václav for the Order of the Poor Clares on request of his sister Agnes, who be-

came the first abbess and was sanctified in 1989. The convent was next to a Minorite monastery. After its dissolution in 1782 the premises deteriorated. Exacting reconstruction work, finished in 1986, adapted St Agnes Convent for the National Gallery in Prague. It houses the collections of Czech 19th century paintings, and concerts, literary evenings and meetings are held here. There is a stylish restaurant in the building. The architecture of St Agnes Convent is a valuable example of Early Gothic of European significance – e. g. the cloister around the Court of Paradise, the Church of St Saviour with the Chapel of Mary Magdalen, the Church of St Francis (the oldest building, of which only the presbytery survives, where the skeletal remains of King Václav I were found). The Gallery is open daily 10 a.m. – 6 p. m. Closed on Monday.

THE JEWISH TOWN – JOSEFOV (Židovské Město)

The smallest of the Prague quarters, Josefov, is surrounded by the Old Town. It can be easily reached from Staroměstská station of Line A of the Metro or from Pařížská Street, which links it with the Old Town Square and Svatopluk Čech Bridge.
Jews settled on the territory of Prague already in the 10th cent. where today Újezd is and below Vyšehrad. Later, probably in the 12th century, another settlement arose in today's Dušní Street around the synagogue called the Old School. This was replaced in the sixties of the 19th cent. by the Spanish Synagogue, whose name derives from the decorations in pseudo-Moorish style made in 1882–1893. In the middle of

The Jewish Town
Josefov (Židovské město)

The Old-New
Synagogue

76

the 13th cent. a Jewish Town grew up around the Old-New Synagogue (Staronová synagoga), and from the 16th cent. this became known as the ghetto. The Jews had their own administration and lived separate from the inhabitants of the Old Town; they were not allowed to take part in political life, suffered programs and several times had to move out of Prague for a time. Despite

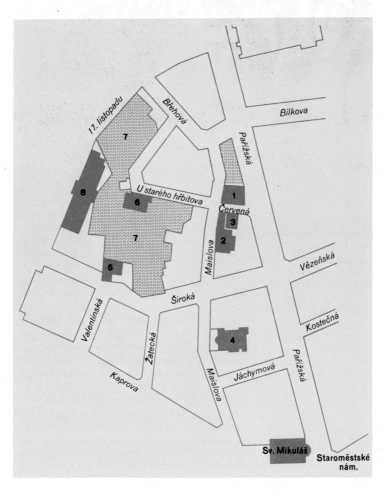

1 The Old–New Synagogue
2 The Jewish Town Hall
3 The High Synagogue
4 The Maisel Synagogue

5 The Pinkas Synagogue
6 The Klausen Synagogue
7 The Old Jewish Cemetery
8 The Museum of Decorative Arts

all these unfavourable events they maintained their own culture. They were given their civic and political rights only in 1848, and in 1850 the Prague ghetto became the fifth Prague quarter known as Josefov in memory of Emperor Joseph II. At the turn of the 19th to 20th century slum clearance removed virtually all the original buildings, and in their place apartment houses in quasi-historical styles were erected. All that remains are the six synagogues, the cemetery and the town hall. This entire complex is unique in Europe, and it is highly frequented. At the corner of Pařížská and Červená stands the most valuable building in Josefov, the **Old-New Synagogue** (Staronová synagoga). (Open April-October 9 a. m. – 6 p. m. November-31 March 9 a. m. – 5 p. m. Closed on Saturday). It is part of the Jewish Museum, which comprises the following: The Old-New Synagogue, one of the oldest Early Gothic buildings in Prague, having been built from the seventies of the 13th cent. Its brick gables date

from the second half of the 15th cent. The oldest part of the synagogue is the entrance lobby with a 17th cent. treasure chest in which the Jewish taxes were collected. A richly decorated portal with tympanum showing motives of vine leaves and grapes leads into the double nave covered with a fivepartite vault resting on six columns. In the centre stands the almemor surrounded by a 15th cent. wrought-iron grille. By the eastern wall there is the shrine with a recess for the torah (the parchment scroll with the Hebrew text of the five Books of Moses). – A statue of Moses by F. Bílek stands in the adjacent little park.

The building of the **High Synagogue** (Vysoká synagoga) on the other side of the narrow Červená Street dates from the second half of the 16th cent., it was enlarged in the nineties of the 17th cent. and adapted in the 19th cent. The large Renaissance hall on the first floor has rich stucco ornamentation and is used for an exhibition of

---

The Jewish Town
Josefov (Židovské město)

The Old Jewish
Cemetery

synagogue textiles (e. g. sanctuary curtains).

The neighbouring **Jewish Town Hall** (Židovská radnice) has a characteristic tower with a clock that has a Hebrew dial. The building was erected at the end of the 16th cent. with funds provided by the mayor of the Jewish Town of Prague, Mordechai Maisel, and was given its present Rococo form after reconstruction in 1763.

These places of interest lie close to the **Old Jewish Cemetery** (Starý židovský hřbitov). Its extensive grounds stretch from Široká Street as far as 17. listopadu Street. On one side it is bordered by the mighty building of the Museum of Decorative Arts. The entrance to the cemetery is to be found at the end of U starého hřbitova Street. It is the most memorable Jewish cemetery in the world. It was founded in the first half of the 15th cent. When the older cemetery in the New Town was closed, certain of the Gothic tombs were brought here. The oldest tomb on the Old Jewish Cemetery is that of Avigdor Kar (1439), the youngest that of Moses Beck (1787). Some 12 000 graves on the grounds of the cemetery form bizarre clusters since older layers of graves were by stages covered with new soil for further graves.

The gravestones were first carved in sandstone, later in white and pink marble, the reliefs on these often recall the names or trade of the deceased. The most famous personality buried on the cemetery is Jehuda ben Becalel, known as Rabbi Löw (died 1609), who, legends relate, created an artificial Man,

the Golem, during the reign of Rudolph II. Since 1975 work has been carried out on the systematic restoration and conservation of the gravestones, and plaques have been affixed to identify the most outstanding personalities. Close to the entrance is the ceremonial hall, built in Neo-Romanesque style in 1906. An exhibition of children's drawings from the concentration camp at Terezín has been installed here.

The Baroque building of the neighbouring **Klausen Synagogue** was erected in 1694. Its main hall, with rich stucco decorations on the vault, houses an exhibition of old Hebrew manuscripts and rare prints, documenting the developed culture of the Jews in Prague and the Czech Lands.

At the southern side of the cemetery, close to the Faculty of Arts, stands the Renaissance **Pinkas Synagogue.** It was founded in the second half of the 15th cent. as a private place for prayers of the Horowitz family and was enlarged in 1535. After the second world war its interior was turned into a Memorial to the Victims of Nazism with 77 297 names of Jews from Bohemia and Moravia who died in concentration camps. The building is again open after undergoing general repairs.

The last building of importance in Josefov is the **Maisel Synagogue** in the street of the same name. The original Renaissance building constructed by Mayor M. Maisel, was altered in Neo-Gothic style in 1892–1905 and is now part of the Jewish Museum. It has a display of silver from Czech synagogues.

The starting point for a walk and the crossroads of most routes to work, shopping and entertainment in the centre of Prague is **Můstek.** In the Middle Ages the walls of the Old Town and the moat lay here. The moat was crossed by a bridge (můstek = bridge) which gave the place its name. The remnants of this bridge can still be seen in the foyer of the Metro station. After the foundation of the New Town in 1348 the walls continued to separate the two towns of Prague, and they were taken down only in the second half of the 18th cent. when the moat was filled in. In recent decades Můstek was a busy crossroad of tram lines and heavy traffic. Now it is a junction of Metro lines A and B and it is the core of the pedestrian zone, the meeting point of Wenceslas Square, Na příkopě Street, Jungmann Square and 28. října Street.

In a south-easterly direction lies the main Prague thoroughfare **Wenceslas Square** (Václavské náměstí).
It is 750 m long and 60 m wide, reminiscent more of a boulevard in Paris than a square. It is the centre of cultural and social life, the main shopping centre, with a number of hotels, restaurants, etc. Car traffic is limited to permit holders. A broad strip with flowerbeds and shrubs stretches down the centre with benches for resting places. Wenceslas Square originated in 1348 when the New Town was founded. At first horse markets were held here and the area bore the name of Horse Market. In the upper section the square ended by the town walls with the Horse Gate (demolished 1875). The square bears the name of Wenceslas Square since 1848. In the 19th and 20th cent. it was the venue of many important

The New Town
Nové Město

Wenceslas
Square

events, assemblies of the people (1848, 1918, 1948, 1968 and most recently the velvet revolution in 1989). From 1680 a statue of St Wenceslas stood in the middle of the square, which was taken to Vyšehrad in 1879. The dominating feature of Wenceslas Square is the Neo-Renaissance building of the **National Museum** (Národní muzeum) at the upper end, built 1885–1890, to plans by J. Schulz. The main front of the museum is over 100 m long. The decorations of the building, the vestibule, staircase, galleries and in particular the dome of the Pantheon illustrate Czech history and the development of science and the arts and introduce leading personalities (painted decorations by J. Mařák, V. Brožík, F. Ženíšek, V. Hynais). From the ramp, above the fountain, decorated with allegorical statues of Bohemia, Moravia, Silesia, the R. Labe and R. Vltava, there is a fine view of the whole

square. Below the Museum, in the upper part of the Square, stands the **St Wenceslas Memorial.** The bronze equestrian statue of 1912 is the work of J. V. Myslbek. Seen from above, from the Museum, on the left-hand side there is the House of Fashion (Dům módy – No. 58, 1954–1956), Phoenix Palace (palác Fénix, No. 56, the work of architect J. Gočár), 1928–1929, in the basement the Blaník Cinema (Kino Blaník), Lucerna Palace (palác Lucerna – No. 38, reached from Štěpánská street No. 61, 1907–1921, a passageway with a cinema and public hall), Wiehl House (Wiehlův dům) No. 34, Neo-Renaissance building with murals designed by M. Aleš and J. Fanta, today Academia Publishing House, Alfa Palace (palác Alfa) No. 28, Constructivist architecture of 1927–1929, with a passageway and access to the Franciscan Garden, Adria Hotel (No. 26, Baroque building of 1784–1789), the

The pedestrian zone
at te bottom
of Wenceslas Square

Baťa Shoe Shop No. 6, Constructivist building of 1928–1929). On the right-hand side there are the following buildings: The White Swan (Bílá labuť) department store –No. 59 of 1959), the Jalta Hotel (No. 45, of 1955–1957), the Europa Hotel (No. 25–27, of 1903–1935), the Krone department store (No. 21, 1976), the Ambassador Hotel (No. 5 of 1912–1913) and Koruna Palace (No. 1, a trade and administrative – building in Art Nouveau style of 1912–1914).

In the upper part of Wenceslas Square there is a pedestrian subway and the Muzeum junction of lines A and C of Prague Metro. In the middle there is an older pedestrian subway (1968, giving access to the Můstek Metro station). It is below the crossing with **Jindřišská Street** with the newly reconstructed Palace Hotel and the Gothic Church of St Henry (kostel sv. Jindřicha) and **Vodičkova Street,** which leads to Charles Square. Another subway is to be found at Můstek.

The National Museum is separated from Wenceslas Square by a busy traffic route, part of the North-South Freeway. Next to it to the north-east stands the former **Federal Assembly** building (1973), in front a sculpture representing the New Era by V. Makovský. The building is now used by Radio Free Europe. The neighbouring building is the **State Opera** Praha, 1886–1888, to plans by the Viennese architects F. Fellner and E. Helmer, reconstructed after 1970; in close vicinity is the Art Nouveau **Main Station** (Praha Hlavní nádraží), 1901–1909, to plans by J. Fanta, sculptural decorations by Č. Vosmík, S. Sucharda, H. Follmann, paintings by J. Fröhlich, modern reconstruction in 1980. It is linked with the Metro station of the same name on line C.

Part of the pedestrian zone in the centre of the city is the short **28. října Street** (ulice 28. října) linking Můstek with Jungmann Square and Národní třída Street, where shops are to be found under the arcades. One of the interesting buildings in Art Nouveau style is No. 13, 1900–1902, where the Publicity Agency Rapid has its offices, and No. 1 is a Constructivist building, dating from 1931, used for offices.

In the centre of **Jungmann Square** stands a statue of J. Jungmann, who was a writer and linguist active in the National Revival Movement last century. A few steps further on is the entrance to the grounds of the **Church of Our Lady-of-the-Snows** (chrám Panny Marie Sněžné). It was founded by Charles IV in 1347, but was never completed. The mighty building that exists is, in fact, the presbytery of a nave and aisles that were never built. The height of the vaulting is 33 m. The construction of the church was interrupted by the Hussite revolution when the church became the centre of the radical wing of the Hussites led by Jan Želivský. From 1603 the church became the property of the Franciscan Order who built a new monastery building, two chapels and the rectory. The Renaissance vaulting of the church is impressive, the Early Baroque altar is the highest in Prague and on the side altar on the left is a valuable picture of the Annunciation by V. V. Reiner of 1724. There is a remarkable portal to the former monastery cemetery with a Gothic tympanum decorated with statues (c. 1346).

Národní Street runs from Jungmann Square in a westerly direction to the R. Vltava. It dates from 1781 when the moat between the Old and the New Town was filled in. On the left-hand side of this main Prague thoroughfare

The New Town
Nové město

stands **Adria Palace** (on the corner of Jungmannova Street) in the style of the Venetian Renaissance palaces (1923–1925). In the passageway there is the Za branou II Theatre. In the neighbouring palace of the Porges of Portheim (No. 38), dating from the late 18th cent, the Russian General Surovov stayed at the time of the Napoleonic Wars in 1799–1800. The Máj department store stands at the corner of Na Perštýně and Spálená Streets (1975). Behind it is the Národní třída Metro station on line B. The Baroque Kaňka House (No. 16) dates from 1735–1740. In the arcades is a plaque in memory of the peaceful demonstration of Prague students on 17 November 1989 which was brutally dispersed by the security forces. It meant the beginning of the "velvet revolution". The Constructivist Danube (Dunaj) Palace, No. 10, was built in 1928–1930. The only sacral buillding on Národní Street is the Church and Convent of the Ursulines from the turn of the 17th to 18th cent., built by architect M. A. Canevalle. Altarpieces by K. Liška, J. R. Byss and P. Brandl. On the ground floor of the convent building is a popular wine cellar.

Národní Street ends with a block of theatre buildings. The **New Theatre** (Nová scéna – 1983) with an original glass front, and an administrative building, a restaurant and the historic Neo-Renaissance **National Theatre** (Národní divadlo). In the centre of the little square is a sculpture by L. Malejovský, and closeby the garden of the Ursuline Convent. The foundation stone to the National Theatre was laid in 1868, and it was originally built to plans by J. Zítek using funds that had been collected by the Czech people. In 1881, shortly before the festive inauguration, the building burnt down. Within two years it was renewed on the basis of plans by J. Schulz, and the festive opening took place in 1883. In the years 1977–1983 extensive reconstruction and modernization was carried out. The most outstanding Czech artists of the time contributed to the decorations of the theatre. The pylons on the main facade support trigas – chariots of the goddess of victory (made to a design by B. Schnirch), the statues of Apollo and the nine Muses on the attic of the loggia are the work of the same artist. The statues above the entrance from the

The National Theatre

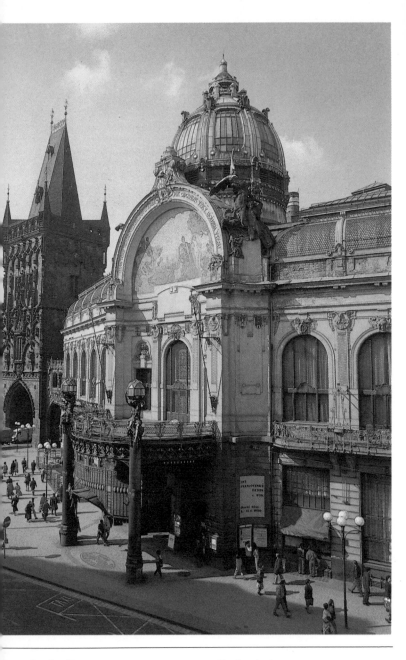

The New Town
Nové Město

The Powder Tower
and the Municipal House

Embankmant (Opera and Drama) were made by J. V. Myslbek. The main foyer is decorated with bronze busts of leading personalities associated with the Czech theatre and opera (J. V. Myslbek, L. Šaloun, S. Sucharda, B. Kafka, J. Štursa, O. Španiel); the cycle of 14 lunettes by M. Aleš depict the theme My Homeland. The mural paintings are by F. Ženíšek. This painter also painted the ceiling of the auditorium. The stage curtain is the work of V. Hynais, who also made the decorations in the Presidential Box.

Opposite the National Theatre is **Slavonic Island** (Slovanský ostrov) and Legion Bridge (Most Legií) linking the town centre with Smíchov and the Lesser Town. The buildings on the right-hand side of **Národní Street** belong to the Old Town but for practical reason are included in this chapter. The most noteworthy are: Platýz (No. 37) with remnants of the wall and bastions in the basement; its present Empire form dates from 1813–1847, when by reconstruction it became the first apartment block in Prague. In 1840 and 1846 F. Liszt gave concerts here (marble bust). The Art Nouveau building (No. 9, formerly Topič Publishers) dates from 1907–1908 and has a richly decorated front with stucco ornaments. The Neo-Renaissance building of the Czech Academy of Sciences (No. 3 and 5) originated in 1858–1862. The neighbouring corner building by Legion Bridge has the famous Slavia coffee-house with views to the Hradčany panorama. It is located in the Neo-Renaissance building of Lažanský Palace (1861–1863).

Na Příkopě Street, leading from Můstek in a north-eastern direction to the Powder Tower, is the busiest section of the pedestrian zone as far as the corner of Panská Street. Like Národní Street it runs along the former moat between the two Prague towns (hence its name "On the Moat"). Buildings along the left-hand, i. e. the Old Town side beginning at Wenceslas Square: a modern office building (No. 1 – 1983) with a large clock and observation coffee-house on the 5th floor, Constructivist building No. 15, (1927–1929), Příkopy Palace (No. 31) with a passageway, the Sevastopol cinema and the mighty building of the Commercial Bank. (1930–1932).

On the right-hand, i. e. the New Town side stand: the House of Elegance (No. 4, 1869–1871), which used to be the oldest department store in town, the Baroque Sylva-Tarroucca Palace (No. 10, 1743–1751, built to plans by K. I. Dientzenhofer and A. Lurago, sculptures by I. F. Platzer), the neighbouring House At the Black Rose (U černé růže – No. 12, Neo-Gothic facade of 1847, passage), the Empire Church of the Holy Rood (kostel sv. Kříže – 1819–1923), part of the adjacent Piarist monastery in Panská Street), the building of the Čedok Travel Agency (No. 18, 1911–1912, with mosaics to a design by J. Preisler), the Živnostenská Bank (No. 20, 1894–1896), built in the style of the Czech Renaissance, with paintings by M. Švabinský in the vestibule), the Neo-Classical Slavonic House (Slovanský dům, No. 22, a cultural and social centre). The last building in Na Příkopě Street, the Czech National Bank (No. 24, 1938), stands on the site of the best-known Prague 19th century hotel where e. g. F. Liszt and F. Chopin stayed. An important junction and point of orientation is **Republic Square** (náměstí Republiky). The Metro station on line B below it has a subway linking it to Masaryk Station. Tram lines cross the square and part of the area is set aside for resting. At the beginning of Celetná Street, at the entrance to the Old Town, stands the **Powder Tower** (see p. 68). Beside it, on the site of the Royal Court, the residence of the Kings of Bohemia from Václav IV to Vladislav II, there now stands the mighty Art Nouveau building of the **Municipal House** (Obecní dům). It was built in the years 1906–1912 to plans by A. Balšánek and O. Polívka. The rich external and interior decorations are the work of leading Czech artists (K. Špillar, L. Šaloun, J. V. Myslbek, M. Švabinský, A. Mucha, M. Aleš, J. Preisler). The Municipal House is the social and cultural centre of the capital city (concerts are held in Smetana Hall, balls, conferences, catering establishments, etc. – At present under major reconstruction. On 28 October 1918 the independence of Czechoslovakia was proclaimed from here. The Empire house **At the Hibernians** (U hybernů) originated 1808-1811 as the result of the rebuilding of the Baroque monastery of the Irish Franciscans as Customs House. The building is now a leading exhibition hall.

On Republic Square there further stands the Kotva department store (1975), a building of 1860 on the site of a former Capuchin monastery, and the Church of St Joseph (1636.1653) with two pictures by K. Škréta. Republic Square is linked with Šverma Bridge and the road tunnel to Letná and Dejvice by **Revoluční Street** lined with shops and office and bank buildings. Kotva Palace (1928) is the head office of Czechoslovak Airlines, Vltava Palace near Šverma Bridge is the air terminal. **Na poříčí** a shopping street, leads from Republic Square to Těšnov where the

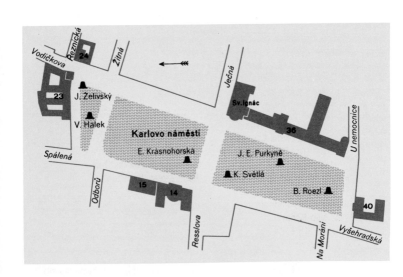

The numbers on the map correspond to those given in the text for each building.

The New Town
Nové Město

largest hotel (Prague Hilton) is located and to Florenc. There is another department store, the White Swan (Bílá labuť – No. 23, 1938) and Axa Palace (1935). The street ends at a crossroad with the flyover of the North-South Freeway. Beyond it the **Museum of the City of Prague** (Muzeum hlavního města Prahy 1896–1898) stands in a little park. The building is Neo-Renaissance in style. Below is the Metro station Florenc on lines B and C with a subway linking it to the Central Bus Terminus Florenc.

Hybernská Street leads from the crossroad at the Powder Tower away from Celetná Street. Since the Middle Ages it has been one of the main thoroughfares of the New Town, with the Hill Gate then standing at its end. Important buildings on Hybernská Street: Saxon Court (Saský dvůr, No. 2, formerly a hotel), Sweerts-Špork Palace (No. 3–5), the "People's House" (Lidový dům), No. 7, the seat of the Czech Social Democratic Party. It is an Early Baroque palace of 1651–1657 to a design by C. Lurago, with Neo-Classical adaptions, Masaryk Station (the oldest in Prague, 1845).

From its foundation **Charles Square** (Karlovo náměstí) was the main square and largest market place of the New Town. Until 1848 it was known as Cattle Market. Since the middle of the 19th cent. its centre is covered by a large park with statues of well-known Czech persons of literature and the natural sciences (E. Krásnohorská, K. Světlá, J. E. Purkyně, B. Roezl). It is connected with Wenceslas Square by the busy Vodičkova Street and another widely used street is Spálená Street with the Máj department store at the corner of Národní Street. The dominating feature of Charles Square is the

New Town Town Hall (Novoměstská radnice, No. 23), which was already in existence in 1377; the entrance hall of columns dates from the early 15th cent., the tower was built 1425–1426, the three gables on the southern front are Renaissance. In 1419 the Hussites led by Jan Želivský threw the New Town Counsellors out of the window of the town hall (Želivský's monument stands in front of the building). In the opposite Baroque Salma House (No. 24) the Czech sculptor M. B. Braun died in 1748. At the corner of Ječná Street stands the Baroque **Church of St Ignatius,** part of the Jesuit college (No. 36) built by C. Lurago in 1665-1670). It has rich stucco decorations and valuable pictures by J. Heintsch and I. Raab. At the corner of Vyšehradská Street is Faust House (Faustův dům – No. 40). In the 16th cent. the English alchemist E. Kelley lived here. – The Neo-Renaissance house No. 14 (on the corner of Charles Square and Resslova Street) built 1867, belongs to the Czech University of Technology. From the centre of

The New
Town Hall

Charles Square **Resslova Street** leads toward the river and Jirásek Bridge. On the right-hand side is the **Church of SS Cyril and Methodius**, a Baroque building of 1730–1736 erected to plans by K. I. Dietzenhofer; it now belongs to the Czechoslovak Orthodox Church. Its crypt was the hiding-place of the parachutists who, in 1942, carried out the assassination of the so-called deputy Reich Protector R. Heydrich; during the last battle here they all lost their lives (memorial plaque). The two characteristic modern steeples belong to the **monastery church At the Slavic Brethren** (Emmaus – kostel Na Slovanech), which was damaged during an air-raid in 1945. They fit well into the panorama of the New Town. The monastery was founded by Charles IV in 1347 and became a famous centre of the Old Slavonic liturgy. The building stands in Vyšehradská Street to the south of Charles Square.

Another remarkable building dating from the time of Charles IV is the **Karlov Church** (Church of the Assumption and Charlemagne) on the southern edge of the New Town. The star vault on an octangular nave is unique in Prague and resembles the funeral church of Charlemagne in Aachen (Germany); Its present form dates from 1575.

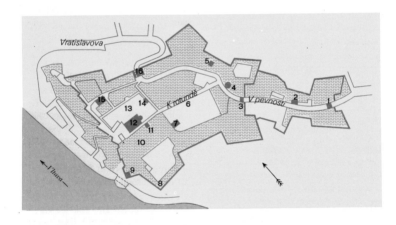

1 The Tábor Gate
2 The Point (Špička) Gate
3 The Leopold Gate
4 The Rotunda of St Martin
5 The Church of St John the Beheaded
6 The New Deanery
7 The Basilica of St Lawrence
8 The former Burgrave's House
9 The ruins of Libuše's bath
10 The statues by Myslbek
11 The remnants of a Romanesque bridge
12 The Church of SS Peter and Paul
13 The Vyšehrad cemetery
14 The Pantheon (Slavín)
15 The New Provost's House
16 The Brick Gate

The New Town
Nové Město

The grounds of Vyšehrad in the southern part of Prague are most easily reached from Vyšehrad Station of line C of Prague Metro, situated on the lower level of the **Nusle Bridge** (Nuselský most) completed in 1973. The bridge links the New Town with Pankrác and forms part of the North-South Freeway, which links up with the motorway Prague-Brno-Bratislava. The bridge is 485 m long, 26 m wide and the average height above the Nusle valley is 40 m. From the parkland terraces close to the Metro station there is a fine view of the Nusle valley, the Karlov church on the opposite side and the town with Prague Castle. Above the station stands the new **Forum Hotel** (1988) and on the other side the **Palace of Culture** (1976–1981). The Palace has a number of large halls (Congress Hall, Conference Hall, etc.) and smaller premises and several restaurants. Conferences and exhibitions are held here and it serves generally for social and cultural events.

In a westerly direction from the Palace lies Vyšehrad; it takes about 15 minutes there on foot and the towers of the Vyšehrad church make orientation easy. In the legends **Vyšehrad**, the Upper Castle, is connected with Princess Libuše, but in reality it originated as a hillfort a little later than Prague Castle (probably in the first half of the 10th cent.). Its advantageous location on a rocky cliff above the R. Vltava contributed to it becoming, for a short time in the second half of the 10th cent., the prince's residence of Boleslav II (the first stone sanctuary, the mint). In the second half of the 11th and the first half of the 12th cent. it was the seat of the Přemyslid princes. This

involved major building activity (stone fortifications, palaces, churches). The significance grew further with the establishment of the Vyšehrad Chapter in 1070, which came to play an important role in the history of Vyšehrad when the sovereign returned to Prague Castle in 1140. Elizabeth of Přemyslid, the mother of Charles IV, spent the last years of her life at Vyšehrad. During the reign of Charles IV new Gothic fortifications were built and the royal palace and the chapter church were reconstructed. Charles' rules for the coronation of the Kings of Bohemia laid down that the ceremonies began at Vyšehrad, from where the Royal Route led through the town to Prague Castle. At the time of the Hussite revolution the Prague Hussites defeated the royal army outside Vyšehrad in 1420 and occupied Vyšehrad. In the second half of the 15th cent. the devastated area was filled with burghers' houses (Town

The Forum Hotel

Vyšehrad –
the Upper Castle

Vyšehrad
and its fortifications

of Mount Vyšehrad). Vyšehrad received its present Baroque form in the middle of the 17th cent. when the town houses were demolished. It served as fort until 1866 and in 1883 it was linked to Prague and became one of its quarters. In the second half of the 19th cent. the old Vyšehrad cemetery was converted into a national cemetery and famous personalities are laid to rest here. In view of the importance of Vyšehrad in the history of the Czech nation extensive archeological research has been carried out and the entire area is undergoing reconstruction.

From the Palace of Culture Vyšehrad can be reached along V pevnosti Street with the **Tábor Gate** at its beginning (1655), which was part of the outer fortifications. The fort itself is entered through the **Leopold Gate** (C. Lurago, 1678) with sculptural decorations. Along its sides stretch Baroque brick walls and originally there was a drawbridge here. A little further along, on the right-hand side is the **Rotunda of St Martin,** the oldest surviving building in Vyšehrad (last third of 11th cent.) and the oldest rotunda in Prague. Its present appearance is the result of building repairs in the last quarter of the 19th cent. The Neo-Romanesque altarpiece was painted by F. Sequens. Behind the rotunda on the left, in K rotundě Street is the **New Deanery** (Nové děkanství – No. 10, built 1877–1879 by J. Niklas). It houses a permanent exhibition of the history of Vyšehrad (open daily 9.30-16.30). Alongside the New Deanery are the houses of the canons of the Vyšehrad Chapter (middle of 19th cent.). At the corner of Soběslav and K rotundě streets stands a Baroque statue of St Adalbert (sv. Vojtěch) in a glass-covered corner chapel (first half of 18th cent.). In Karlach Park on

the right a "Devils' Column" (Čertův sloup) has stood since 1888. It is likely to be a remnant of the ancient Romanesque basilica from the 11th or 12th cent.

The little Neo-Romanesque **Chapel of St Ludmila** close to the entrance to the Church of SS Peter and Paul dates from 1885 (A. Baum), inside is a statue of St Ludmila by M. J. Brokoff, 1718.

The Baroque building of the **Old Provosts' House** (Staré proboštství) (No. 1) was built as residence of the provosts of Vyšehrad in c. 1719. The Neo-Gothic **New Provosts' House** (Nové proboštství, No. 4) has a richly decorated oriel chapel above the entrance portal.

In **Štulc Park** in front of the New Provosts' House stands an equestrian statue of St Wenceslas (J. J. Bendl, 1678) on an Empire pedestal by J. Kranner (1827). It was brought here from Wenceslas Square in 1879 (now copy, the original is in the National Gallery). Nearby is the Václav Štulc monument, the provost of the Vyšehrad Chapter (1814–1887), who was responsible for the establishment of the national cemetery.

St Martin's
Rotunda

(The monument was made by Š. Zálesák in 1910). Below Štulc Park a Summer Theatre (Letní scéna) has been established inside the fortifications where performances are given from May until October.

The main entrance to the Vyšehrad cemetery is to be found by the side of the Church of SS Peter and Paul. The cemetery is open from 8.00–18.00, in winter from 9.00–16.00.

The **Vyšehrad cemetery** (Vyšehradský hřbitov) is one of the main sights of Prague. It became a national cemetery thanks to the patriotic provosts V. Štulc and M. Karlach. The first gravestones were made by A. Barvitius who was followed in 1898–1908 by A. Wiehl. There is a unique gallery of funeral sculpture associated with other famous names (J. V. Myslbek, B. Kafka, O. Španiel, K. Lidický and others). Some 600 personalities in Czech national culture are buried here (e. g. the writers and poets E. Bass, K. Čapek with his wife, the actress and writer O. Scheinpflugová, Sv. Čech, F. Hrubín, K. H. Mácha, J. Neruda, B. Němcová, V. Nezval, painters M. Aleš, A. Chittussi, K. Purkyně. M. Švabinský, sculptors V. Levý, O. Španiel, composers A. Dvořák, Z. Fibich, B. Smetana, scientists J. Heyrovský, J. E. Purkyně). A part of the cemetery is formed by the Pantheon (Slavín) built 1889–1893), to a design by A. Wiehl, with sculpture by J. Maudr, a bronze cross by V. Levý. It is the common tomb of more than 50 outstanding personalities (J. Zeyer, J. Vrchlický, V. Hynais, A. Mucha, V. Špála, J. V. Myslbek, J. Štursa, B. Kafka, E. Destinová, Z. Štěpánek, E. Kohout, F. Křižík, etc.).

The **Church of SS Peter and Paul** (Kostel svatého Petra a Pavla) rises next to the cemetery. It is a Romanesque basilica by origin, built by Vratislav II in

1070–1080 in connection with the establishment of the Vyšehrad Chapter. The crypt is the burial place of Přemyslid rulers Vratislav II, Konrad, Soběslav I and Soběslav II. After a fire the basilica was re-built; during the reign of Charles IV a Gothic church was built, adapted in Renaissance style in the 16th cent. and with Baroque alterations in 1707–1729 (F. M. Kaňka, C. Canevalle). Its present Neo-Gothic form with the two towers dates from 1885–1903 (J. Mocker, F. Mikeš). The high altar was designed by J. Mocker (1884). The Neo-Gothic windows in the presbytery were decorated by F. Sequens as were the mosaic windows in the side chapels; the statue of Christ by the triumphal arch is the work of Č. Vosmík. All that survives of the original furnishings are the canons' pews in the presbytery (end of 17th cent.) and the pews in the nave date from the same period. The church has a Romanesque stone sarcophagus from c. 1 100, probably the

---

Vyšehrad –
the Upper Castle

The Pantheon (Slavín)
on the Vyšehrad Cemetery

tomb of a Přemyslid prince (first side chapel on the right). There is a Gothic votive picture of the Madonna of Vyšehrad from the period after 1350 (on the altar in the third chapel on the right). From the church a Baroque portal (1655) leads into **Vyšehrad park**. The portal, originally part of the armoury, was transferred to this place in 1927. In the park are **statues of the legendary figures** in Czech history (Lumír and the Song, Záboj and Slavoj, Ctirad and Šárka, Přemysl and Libuše – by J. V. Myslbek, 1881–1897) brought here from the bridge-ends of Palacký Bridge in 1948. The park, laid out in 1927, used to be the original prince's and royal acropolis. Part of the royal palace from the time of Charles IV has survived in the building of the Burgrave's House (No. 973), altered in the 16th cent. West of it there are further remnants of the medieval buildings and the castle tower dating back to the 11th cent. The tower, adapted in Baroque, houses the Vyšehrad Gallery (open Tuesday-Sunday, 9.30–17.00). From the western edge of the bastion there is a fine view over the Vltava and the Prague basin.

The eastern part of the park is formed by Soběslavova Street, where near the Old Deanery (No. 1.), behind the Neo-Romanesque portal, there are the foundations of an Early Romanesque **Basilica of St Lawrence** (bazilika sv. Vavřince) from the end of the 11th cent. (open daily 10.00–16.00).

The street continues along the southern fortifications with a view over the Vltava and the southern parts of Prague. Below the walls is a big building of the Podolí Sanatorium.

The street links up with V pevnosti Street which takes us back to the Palace of Culture or can be followed to the left along the northern fortifications, where it ends in the **Brick/Chotek/Gate** (Cihelna) that links Vyšehrad with the New Town. It was erected in 1841–1842 by Governor K. Chotek. A permanent exhibition of the Vyšehrad Fortress in the History of Prague Fortifications has been established in the gateway. (open daily 9.30–16.30). There, too, is the entrance to the casemates. From the Gate the way leads down to Rašín Embankment and the tram stop.

OTHER PLACES OF INTEREST IN PRAGUE

Bertramka, W. A. Mozart Memorial, address: Mozartova Street, Prague 5 Smíchov, not far from the Anděl station of Line B of Prague Metro. Originally a 17th century suburban homestead where Mozart stayed during his visits to Prague in 1787 and 1791. His hosts and close friends were the owners, composer and pianist František Xaver Dušek and his wife Josefína, an outstanding singer of the time. The house is furnished in end of 18th century style and houses a number of items, among

Břevnov Abbey

them the piano and harpsichord, on which Mozart played in Prague. In summer concerts of classical music are given in the building and the garden.

Břevnov, an extensive Benedictine Abbey in Prague 6 Břevnov, Markétská Street 28. Can be reached from the Hradčanská station of Line A of Prague Metro by tram. The Abbey was founded in 993 as the first monastery in Bohemia. It was given its present Baroque form by K. Dientzenhofer in 1700–1720. Valuable paintings from c. 1740. K. Dientzenhofer built another important building on the grounds of the monastery, the Church of St Margaret (kostel sv. Markéty) in the years 1708–1715. A pre-Romanesque crypt from the early 11th century has recently been uncovered below the choir of the church.

Exhibition Ground (Výstaviště), in Prague 7 Holešovice, not far from the Nádraží Holešovice Metro station on Line C. Established as a centre for entertainment and culture in 1952. Programs include exhibitions, fairs, sport, cultural performances, and an amusement park for children. The main building is pseudo-Baroque, a ferro-concrete building of the Industrial Palace of 1891, where congresses and exhibitions are held. The modern sports hall with 17 000 seats is set aside chiefly for winter sports. In a separate circular pavilion there is a panoramatic picture by painter and graphic artist L. Marold (1865–1898) showing the Battle of Lipany on an area of one thousand square metres. It refers to the tragic battle in 1434 in which the radical wing of the Hussite army was finally defeated. – In close vicinity stands the one-time Trade Fair Palace of 1924–1928, which is

used by the National Gallery in Prague for its Collections of 20th Century Art. **Letná Park** (Letenské sady) in Prague 7 was laid out after the middle of the 19th century. It provides opportunities for rest and unusual views over historic Prague. An interesting viewpoint can be gained from the Praha Expo 58 restaurant, which was transferred here from the World Exhibition in Brussels, where it reaped great success. Interesting views can be had also from the open space from which the Stalin Statue was removed. An uncommon building in the park is the Hanau Pavilion, built for the Jubilee Exhibition in 1891 and later brought here. Many visitors are interested in the National Technical Museum (Národní technické museum) in adjacent Kostelní Street 42 with interesting exhibits of vintage cars, motorcycles as well as astronomical and optical apparatuses.

Olšany Cemetery (Olšanské hřbitovy). Entrance from Vinohradská Street (Flora or Želivského stations of Line A of Prague Metro). Established in 1680,

Second World War. The writer Franz Kafka is buried on the Jewish cemetery.

Star Summer Palace (Letohrádek Hvězda) in a one-time deer-park lies on the western edge of Prague. It can be reached from the Hradčanská station of Line A of Prague Metro by tram to the terminus Horní Liboc-Petřiny. The palace was built in the years 1555–1556 in Renaissance style on a ground plan of a five-pointed star. The deer-park was turned into a park in the 19th century and nowadays serves for recreation and sport (jogging, skiing). The palace houses a museum devoted to the work of a leading Czech writer of historical novels Alois Jirásek (1851–1930) and to Mikoláš Aleš (1852–1913), a well-known painter of pictures of Bohemian history. Not far from the park was the site of the Battle of the White Mountain in 1620, which had tragic consequences in Czech history. A small monument

the main Prague cemetery since 1784. Graves of important personalities of Czech culture and public life, with tombstones of considerable sculptural value. Burial place of the Red Army soldiers who laid down their lives in the liberation of Prague in May 1945 (enormous monument). The cinerarium of British airmen who died in Bohemia during the

The Star
Summer Palace

Troja
Chateau

marks the site. Not far from the tram terminus is a Baroque pilgrims' Chapel of Our Lady Victorious (kaple P. Marie Vítězné).

Stromovka Park, Prague 7, is an extensive public park, once a royal deer-park, established already during the reign of King Přemysl Otakar II. It is widely used by the people of Prague for walks and rest. A footbridge across Imperial Island leads to the chateau of Troja and the Zoo.

Troja, Baroque chateau in Prague 7, which can be reached by bus from the Holešovické nádraží station of Line C of Prague Metro or on foot from Stromovka Park. The first Baroque residence in Prague built to plans by J. B. Mathey in the years 1679–1685. Monumental garden stairway with statues of ancient gods by the Dresden artists J. J. and P. Hermann. Now art gallery. Not far away is the Prague Zoological Garden, established 1931 in a fine natural setting close to the R. Vltava. Among its most precious animals is the Przewalski's horse.

Zbraslav, now part of Prague 5, but until recently a separate township south of Prague close to the confluence of the R. Berounka and the Vltava. Large monastery complex founded by King Václav II in 1292 under the Latin name of Aula regia. The last Přemyslid kings are buried in the local Church of St Mary.

The buildings were reconstructed in Baroque style in the first half of the 18th century to plans by J. B. Santini and F. M. Kaňka. The monastery was dissolved in 1784 and turned into a chateau. It now houses the Collections of Czech 19th and 20th Century Sculpture of the National Gallery in Prague.

Žižkov, National Memorial on Žižkov Hill (formerly Vítkov) dominating the Prague Basin. Can be reached on foot or by bus from the Florenc Station of Lines B or C of Prague Metro. It was on this site that the Hussite armies under Jan Žižka defeated the Crusaders in 1420. In 1929–1932 the mighty building of the Memorial was built of granite. In front stands an equestrian statue of Jan Žižka (height 9 m, sculptor B. Kafka) and the Tomb of the Unknown Soldier. View over the historical centre of Prague.

THE ENVIRONS OF PRAGUE

In the surroundings of Prague are many places of interest. This is particularly true of the southern approaches where there is undulating country covered with woodlands and broken up by the deep valley of the R. Vltava (with a series of reservoirs and dams), the R. Berounka and the R. Sázava. These areas are popular with the people of Prague and are used for recreational purposes. To the north of the capital city the R. Vltava flows into the fertile lands along the R. Labe (Elbe) and joins it at the confluence in Mělník. Numerous castles, chateaux, churches, monasteries and historical towns are scattered throughout Central Bohemia, and there are many interesting museums and art galleries. The following selection (given in alphabetical order) mentions only the most important places that can be reached in full-day or half-day excursions.

Český Šternberk, village and castle 50 km south-east of Prague in the recreation area along the R. Sázava. Originally Gothic castle from c. 1240 on the left bank of the R. Sázava, later re-built in Late Gothic and then Early Baroque style, its present appearance dating from c. 18th century. Collections of armoury, 17th century graphic art and period furniture.

Karlstein Castle (Karlštejn), Gothic castle on a rocky hill above the valley of the R. Berounka, 31 km south-west of Prague. The castle was built by Emperor Charles IV in 1348–1357 for safekeeping of the imperial Crown Jewels and relics of Saints. In 1420 King Sigismund removed the imperial jewels but the Bohemian Crown Jewels were kept here until 1619. After the Thirty Years' War the castle lost its importance and became a popular destination for trips in the first half of the 19th century. Restored 1887–1899. At the highest point of the castle stands a mighty square tower with the Holy Rood Chapel (Kaple sv. Kříže). The walls of the chapel are inlaid with semi-precious stones and are hung with 127 paintings of Saints by Master Theodoric (1348–1367). (At present closed to the public). Emperor Charles IV often stayed in the residential palace, which is now a museum. In the central tower is the Lady Chapel (kaple P. Marie) with a set of Gothic paintings including portraits of the founder of the castle. The adjacent St. Catherine's Chapel (kaple sv. Kateřiny) has walls adorned with semi-precious stones and paintings and was

Karlštejn
Castle

the Emperor's private oratory.

The castle is surrounded by a Protected Landscape Area known as **Czech Karst** with forests, limestone rocks, caves. 7 km to the south-west lie the **Koněprusy Caves** (Koněpruské jeskyně) with rich stalagmites and stalactites, which are open to the public.

Kokořín Castle, Gothic, first half of 14th century, in a picturesque location on a sandstone rock above the Kokořín valley, 13 km north of Mělník and 45 km north of Prague. Adapted in 1911–1916 by the last owner. It has two main features: a round tower with a cone-shaped helmet and a palace. Around the castle lies the Kokořín Protected Landscape Area with interesting rock formations and sandstone valleys. 2 km to the north-east are the Pokličky mushroom-shaped rock formations (parking place along the road in the direction of Duba). Vernacular architecture.

Kolín, district town in the fertile Labe (Elbe) Valley, 56 km east of Prague. Founded as a royal town in 1257. The town centre is a Historic Town Reserve. The most outstanding among other old buildings is the Early Gothic Church of St Bartholomew (kostel sv. Bartoloměje). The nave dates from the second half of the 13th century and in 1360–1378 the choir was built by Petr Parler, who built the Prague St Vitus' Cathedral. The belfry was erected in 1504. Originally Gothic town hall, its present appearance from 1887. Baroque houses. 15th century Jewish cemetery. Every year in June the town is the venue of a brass band festival.

Konopiště Chateau, on the edge of the district town of Benešov, 45 km south of Prague. Originally a French type castle with four towers dating from c. 1300, many times rebuilt. The present chateau was given its form in 1889–

1894 when it belonged to the successor to the Austro-Hungarian throne Ferdinand d'Este. In 1924 a secret meeting with the German Emperor Wilhelm was held here. Valuable collections, e.g. armour (4 682 items) and statues and pictures of St George, etc. English park with a rose garden and sculpture brought from Italy. – 6 km to the north in **Poříčí nad Sázavou** two little Romanesque churches: a cemetery Church of St Peter with a tribune from the late 11th century and the Church of St Gall (kostel sv. Havla) from the early 13th century, with later adaptations.

Křivoklát Castle in a picturesque position on a promontory above the valley of the Rakovník Stream close to its confluence with the R. Berounka, 55 km west of Prague. By the early 12th century a wooden hunting lodge of the Bohemian princes stood on this site, re-built as stone castle in the middle of the 13th century. King Charles IV stayed here in 1319–1323 and 1333. Several Gothic alterations during the reign of Wladislav II, 1471–1516. In the 16th century the castle was used as prison.

The dominant feature of the castle is the 32 m high round tower, built in the 13th century, with the palace between it and the square Huderka tower. Exhibition of the castle history, the queen's chambers, the library, Late Gothic sculpture and paintings. The chapel has a valuable altar, there is a 40 m deep well, in the prison medieval torture instruments. Exhibition devoted to the Křivoklát Protected Landscape Area, an extensive territory of deciduous and mixed forests along the middle course of the R. Berounka, formerly the hunting grounds of the Bohemian monarchs.

Kutná Hora, district town, 65 km east of Prague where the fertile lowlands turn into an undulating landscape. In the Middle Ages the second most important town in Bohemia, the temporary seat of the Kings of Bohemia. The town grew up in the 13th century close to rich silver mines. The profits from the mines made the Bohemian Kings for a time some of the richest monarchs in Europe. A mint was established in 1300, where the Bohemian (Prague) Groschen were coined. At the turn of the 14th to 15th century Kutná Hora was the favourite residence of King Václav IV. Income from the mines decreased in the 16th century, the last Bohemian Groschen was coined in 1547. The mint was closed in 1726. The town had a rich cultural life and a number of writers lived here. Historical Town Reserve: The dominant feature is the church of St Barbara (chrám sv. Barbory), the patron saint of miners, built in the years 1388-1565 by the leading Bohemian architects of the Gothic period (masonic lodge of P. Parler, M. Rejsek, B. Ried). Net vaulting, coats-of-arms, Gothic frescoes, paintings. Gothic church of St James (kostel sv. Jakuba), 1330–1420, with a 82 m high steeple, pictures by P. Brandl and K. Škréta. The Italian Court (Vlašský dvůr) was a royal residence and mint. As a Gothic building with chapel and tower it dates from 1296–1299. Valuable Gothic rooms are open to the public. The Small Fort (Hrádek) founded after 1300 was part of the town fortifications; its present appearance is Late Gothic from the 15th century. In the Knights' Hall are Gothic frescoes and the building now serves as museum of mining and minting. Burghers' houses were re-built as the Stone House (Kamenný dům) of 1485

The interior
of Konopiště Chateau

Křivoklát
Castle

with oriels and a richly decorated front, the Prince's House (Knížecí dům) of c. 1500 and Šultys House (Šultysův dům). There are several other churches and monasteries, with an interesting exhibition of arts and crafts in the Ursuline Convent, and a Jesuit College with a gallery of sculptures in front of the main facade. A twelve-sided Late Gothic stone fountain of 1493–1495 (M. Rejsek), pest column of 1713–1715. In the **Sedlec** district there is a large monastery founded in 1142. A Gothic church with nave and double aisles of 1290–1330, adapted in Baroque with paintings by P. Brandl. 400 m away there is a cemetery chapel with an ossuary (containing bones of about 10 000 persons). 3 km from the centre is **Kaňk Hill** (352 m) with tailings and caved-in tunnels left from medieval mining.

Lány, remarkable chateau set in a park near extensive woodlands and a deer-park with deer and stags, 40 km from Prague. Originally Renaissance, used by Emperor Rudolph II when hunting in the local woods. After a number of alterations it was adapted in 1921 as the summer residence of the Presidents of the Czechoslovak Republic (architect J. Plečník). In the park is a large greenhouse with palmtrees. The first Czech President Thomas Garrigue Masaryk is buried on the local cemetery.

Lidice, a village 30 km west of Prague, the symbol of the struggle against fascism. The village was levelled to the ground by the Gestapo on 10 June 1942 and all 192 men were shot at the Horák homestead. 196 women and 105 children were taken to concentration camps. The reason given was alleged contact between two of the local families and the men who assassinated the German "Protector" R. Heydrich. The entire area is now a National Cultural

Monument. There is a museum relating the events and a Rose Garden of Friendship and Peace.

Mělník, district town in fertile agricultural land 33 km north of Prague. A chateau stands on a high hill above the confluence of the rivers Labe and Vltava, and the southern slopes are covered with vineyards. The history of Mělník goes back to the 10th century, when a castle of the Slavic Pshovans stood on this site. Royal town from 1274 in which the queens took up residence on many occasions until 1475. Emperor Charles IV encouraged the layout of vineyards for which he brought Burgundy vines.

The chateau was built on the site of the Romanesque and Gothic castle and a Renaissance wing was added with later Baroque adaptations. The chateau houses a museum with an exposition of viniculture, a picture gallery with works of the leading masters of Baroque (P. Brandl, K. Škréta, V. V. Reiner), and a renowned wine-cellar. In close vicinity stands the Gothic Church of SS Peter and Paul, with a high steeple, its present appearance dating from the late 15th and early 16th century with valuable furnishings and an ossuary. The square is surrounded by houses with arcades, most outstanding among them

---

The chateau at Lány

the Baroque town hall with a Gothic core. The Prague Gate survives of the medieval fortifications.

Nelahozeves, 26 km north of Prague. Renaissance chateau from the years 1553–1593, built on a rock above the left bank of the R. Vltava. Now houses the Central Bohemian Art Gallery (Středočeská gallerie) with collections of Old European Art. The halls are furnished in 16th-17th century style and include an exhibition of armoury. In the village is the birthplace of Antonín Dvořák (1841–1904), now a museum devoted to the composer and his work.

Poděbrady, spa town on the R. Labe 48 km east of Prague. Treats diseases of the heart and blood circulation. Colonnade, park, 13 mineral springs (at a depth of 86–105 m). Bohemia Glass-Works (lead crystal glass). On the banks of the river stands a mighty chateau with a round tower, which belonged to King George of Poděbrady, whose equestrian statue stands in the middle of the square.

Sázava, town and summer resort 45km south-east of Prague on the R. Sázava. Kavalier Glass-Works (laboratory and heat-resisting glassware), with a tradition dating back to the first half of the 19th century. – Monastery founded by Prince Oldřich in c. 1032. The monks used the Slavonic liturgy and the first abbot was St Procopius.

A 1350 Chapter Hall with frescoes survives. The monastery church was built throughout the 14th century, but remain-

ed unfinished. In 1785 the monastery was adapted as chateau after its dissolution. Open to the public, exhibition of Slavonic community of Sázava and museum of technical glassware.

Slapy, village and summer resort 30 km south of Prague. Closeby is the Slapy Dam on the R. Vltava, built 1950–1954, 65 m high, holding a reservoir 44 km long with an area of 1392 hectares. Extensive recreation area, with weekend houses, boat trips, aquatic sports and bathing.

Veltrusy, chateau 27 km north of Prague on the R. Vltava, built in the first half of the 18th century. The great hall extends through both storeys and has a dome above it. Valuable furnishings in the state rooms. English park 300 ha in size, with Empire and romantic buildings.

The sphinx in the chateau park at Veltrusy

PRACTICAL INFORMATION

It would take several full days to visit all the museums and art galleries in Prague, which number more than thirty. The following brief survey with characteristic features of exhibits and practical information on routes and opening hours will help visitors to plan their programme in our capital city.

National Museum (Národní muzeum), Václavské náměstí 68, P. 1 - Nové Město.
Route: Metro Lines A and C, Muzeum station.
Opening hours: Daily except Tuesdays 9-17, Wednesdays until 9 p. m. The Museum was established in 1818, its present monumental building from the late 19th century stands at the top of Wenceslas Square. The ground floor is reserved for temporary exhibitions. First floor: mineralogy, petrographic exhibition (minerals from the whole world, meteorites), pre-historic development on Czechoslovak territory, numismatic collections, modern history from the middle 19th century to the present. On the second floor: seven halls of zoological exhibitions, including a whale skeleton and paleontological exhibitions. Concerts are regularly held on the stairway.
The National Museum has a number of specialized departments and certain exhibits are on display in other than the main building.

National History Museum (Památky národní minulosti). History exhibition of the National Museum, Lobkowicz Palace, Jiřská, P. 1 - Hradčany.
Route: Metro Line A, Malostranská station, up the Old Castle steps (Staré zámecké schody) to Prague Castle.

*Museums
and Galleries*

Opening hours: Daily except Mondays, 9–17 hrs.
A modern exhibition in the historic halls of the 16th-18th century palace. Gives insight into the history of the Czech Lands and Slovakia from the beginings of feudalism to the revolutionary year 1848. Exact copies of the royal Crown Jewels are on display.

Ethnographical Museum (Národopisné muzeum), Petřínské sady 98, P. 5-Smíchov.
Route: Metro Line B, Anděl station, tram and bus stop náměstí Kinských.
Opening hours: At present closed for reconstruction.
The museum is sited in the Empire Kinský villa. The most complete ethnographical exhibition in Czechoslovakia.

Bedřich Smetana Exhibition (Muzeum Bedřicha Smetany), part of the Museum of Czech Music, Novotného lávka 1, P. 1 – Staré Město.
Route: Metro Line A, Staroměstská station, then along Křižovnická Street past Charles Bridge.
Opening hours: At present closed for reconstruction.
The exhibition is devoted to the founder of modern Czech music (his life, correspondence, manuscript scores).

Antonín Dvořák Exhibition (Muzeum Antonína Dvořáka), part of the Museum of Czech Music, Ke Karlovu 20, P. 2 – Nové Město.
Route: Metro Line C, I. P. Pavlova station.
Opening hours: Daily except Mondays, 10–17.
Located in the Baroque Michna summer palace, also known as Villa America, built 1712–1720 to plans by K. I. Dientzenhofer. Devoted to the life and work of the famous composer.

W. A. Mozart and the Dušeks' Muzeum (Památník W. A. Mozarta a manželů Duškových), Bertramka, Mozartova 169, P. 5 – Smíchov.
Route: Metro Line B, Anděl station.
Opening hours: Daily except Tuesdays, 9.30–6.00 p. m.
The museum is housed in the Bertramka homestead from the second half of the 17th century, where Mozart stayed during his visits to Prague in 1787 and 1791. His hosts were the composer F. X. Dušek and his wife J. Dušková, a famous singer. Mozart composed his opera Don Giovanni here. Concerts of classical music are given here.

Tyrš Museum of Physical Culture and Sport, Újezd 40, P. 1 – Malá Strana
Route: tram stop Karmelitská.
Opening hours: Daily except Mondays 9-5 p. m. Sundays from 10 a. m.
The museum is situated in Tyrš House. History of physical culture and sport on the territory of the former Czechoslovakia. Collection of medals and trophies belonging to Czech sportsmen. Souvenirs of the nation-wide Sokol festivals.

Náprstek Museum of Asian, African and American Cultures (Náprstkovo muzeum), Betlémské náměstí 1, P. 1 – Staré Město.
Route: Metro Line B, Národní třída station.
Opening hours: Daily except Mondays, 9–12, 12.45–17.30.

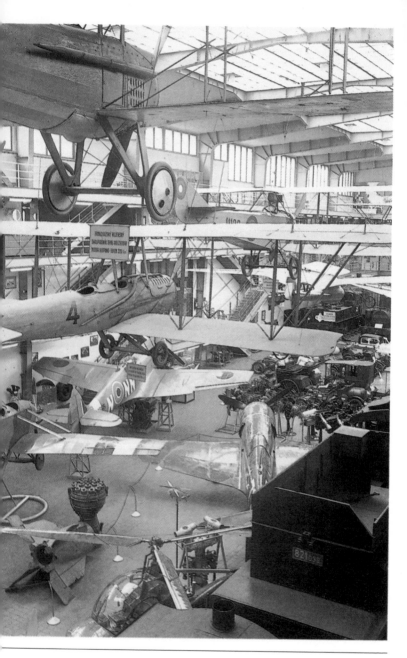

Collections of exhibits of the cultures of the original inhabitants of Africa, America, Oceania. The exhibition of Asian cultures is situated in the chateau of Liběchov near Mělník.

National Technical Museum (Národní technické muzeum), Kostelní 42, P.7 – Holešovice.
Route: Metro Line A, Hradčanská station, on foot through Letná Park, by tram to Letenské náměstí.
Opening hours: Daily except Mondays, 9–17.
The building of 1939-1942 houses collections that document the history of the railway, road traffic, the aeroplane and ship transport; a mechanized coal and ore mine deserves attention, astronomical and surveying apparatuses, exhibitions in the field of film and photographic technology, etc.

Toy Museum, Old Burgrave's House (Staré purkrabství), Jiřská 4, P. 1 – Hradčany.
Route: Metro Line A, Malostranská station. Up the Old Castle Steps (Staré zámecké schody) to Prague Castle.
Opening hours: Daily 9.30–5.30 p. m.
One of the largest toy exhibitions in the world, the oldest toys dating from ancient Greece.

Historical Exhibition of the Military Museum (Historická expozice Vojenského muzea), Hradčanské náměstí 2, P. 1 – Hradčany.
Route: Metro Line A, Malostranská station, on foot through Prague Castle, or tram stop Pohořelec or Hrad.
Opening hours: 1 May–31 October daily except Mondays 10 a. m. – 6 p. m.
The exhibition is housed in the Renaissance Schwarzenberg Palace and gives a picture of the military history on the territory of the Czech Republic.

Jewish Museum (Židovské muzeum), Jáchymova 3, P. 1 – Josefov.
Route: Metro Line A, Staroměstská station.
Opening hours: 1 April–31 October, daily except Saturdays 9–18, 1 November-31 March to 5 p. m.
The museum was established in 1950 in the area that used to be the Prague ghetto.
The exhibitions are held in the historic synagogues: (the High, Klausen, Pinkas and Spanish synagogues), and include synagogal textiles, objects of silver, etc.

Museum of Decorative Arts (Uměleckoprůmyslové muzeum), ulice 17. listopadu 2, P. 1 – Staré Město.
Route: Metro Line A, Staroměstská station.
Opening hours: Daily except Mondays 10–18.
The museum exhibitions give a survey of the development of arts and crafts. The collection of glassware is one of the most beautiful in the world.

Museum of the City of Prague (Muzeum hlavního města Prahy), Na Poříčí, P. 2 – Nové Město.
Route: Metro Lines B and C, Florenc station.
Opening hours: daily except Mondays, 10 a.m. – 6 p.m.
The exhibits centre on the historical development of Prague, archeology, history and decorative arts. Langweil's model of Prague in the first half of the 19th century. Part of the

museum collections is the exhibition of the history of Vyšehrad (K rotundě Street 10, P. 2 – Vyšehrad) and the exhibition of old Podskalí at Výtoň (Rašínovo nábřeží 412, P. 2 – Nové Město – open only in summer).

Postage Stamp Museum (Muzeum poštovní známky), Nové mlýny 2, P. 1 – Nové Město.
Route: Metro Line B, Náměstí Republiky station, tram and bus stop Revoluční.
Opening hours: daily except Mondays 9–17.
Located in Vávra House (a former mill) with wall paintings by J. Navrátil (1847). Philatelist exhibition opened on the occasion of the Philately Exhibition Praga 88.

National Gallery in Prague (Národní galerie v Praze)
Opening hours: All collections are open daily except Mondays 10–18.

Collection of Old Bohemian Art (Sbírka starého českého umění) St George's Convent (Jiřský klášter), Jiřské náměstí, P. 1 – Hradčany.
Route: Metro Line A, Malostranská station. Located in the convent founded in 973. Romanesque art, Gothic sculpture (St. George), painting (Master Theodoric, Master of the Třeboň Altarpiece) etc., Mannerist art of the Rudolphinian period, Czech Baroque painting (Brandl, Kupecký) and sculpture (Brokoff, Braun).

Collection of 19th Century Czech Painting (Sbírka českého malířství 19. stol.).
St Agnes Convent (Anežský klášter), U milosrdných Street 17, P. 1 – Staré Město.
Route: Metro Line B, Náměstí Republiky station. Renovated Gothic building. Includes works by Navrátil, Mánes, Aleš, Brožík, etc.

Collections of 20th Century Art (Sbírky umění 20. stol.). Trade Fair Palace (Veletržní palác) P. 7 – Holešovice, includes modern French art (Cézanne, Gauguin, Monet, Manet, Van Gogh, Matisse, Picasso, Chagall, etc.).

Collection of European Art (Sbírka evropského umění), Sternberg Palace, Hradčanské náměstí 15, P. 1 – Hradčany.
Route: Metro Line A Malostranská or Hradčanská stations.
The largest exhibition of European art in the Czech Republic, with important collections of Dutch and Flemish art (Rembrandt, Rubens, Brueghel).

Collection of Modern Czech Sculpture (Sbírka moderního českého sochařství), P. 5 – Zbraslav.
Route: Bus from Metro Station Anděl of Line B. Exhibition of 19th and 20th century sculpture (Myslbek, Štursa, Bílek).

Chateau Troja, Trojská, P. 7.
Route: By bus from the Metro station Nádraží Holešovice on Line C, terminus at the Zoo.
Opening hours: 1 April – 31 October daily 10 a. m. –5 p. m. Closed on Mondays. Otherwise only Saturday 10 a. m. – 5 p. m.
Baroque chateau built 1679-1685. Permanent exhibition of 19th century Czech art and European faience.

---

*Museums
and Galleries*

Lapidarium of the National Museum. Exhibition Ground (Výstaviště). P. 7 – Holešovice.
Route: Metro Line C, Holešovice station. Tram stop Výstaviště.
Onening hours: Daily except Mondays, 12–17. Saturday and Sunday from 10 a. m. (Midday break).
Collection of Czech sculpture and stonemason work of the 11th to 19th century.

House At the Black Mother of God, Ovocný trh 19, P. 1 – Old Town.
Route: Metro Line B, Náměstí Republiky station.
Opening hours: Daily 10 a. m. – 6 p. m. Closed on Mondays.
Permanent exhibition of Czech Cubism and temporary exhibitions.

Strahov Picture Gallery, Strahovské nádvoří, P. 1 – Hradčany
Route: Tram stop Pohořelec.
Opening hours: Daily 9–12, 12.30–17. Closed on Mondays.
Gothic painting (Madonnas), painting from the period of Rudolph II, Baroque and Rococo painting.

EXHIBITION HALLS

Temporary exhibitions are held in the above museums and art galleries. Detailed information can be found in the daily press, in the booklet Cultural programmes in Prague and on posters in the streets. The following is a selection of other exhibition halls:
Riding School of Prague Castle (Jízdárna Pražského Hradu), U Prašného mostu, P. 1. Exhibition of paintings.
Route: On the approach to the Castle from the tram stop Hrad.
Wallenstein Riding School (Valdštejnská jízdárna), Klárov, P. 1 – Malá Strana. Exhibitions of the fine arts.
Route: Metro Line A, Malostranská station.
U Hybernů, náměstí Republiky, P. 1 – Nové Město. Empire building, one-time church. Well-known Prague exhibition hall.
Kinský Palace, Staroměstské náměstí 12, P. 1 – Old Town, in particular exhibitions of graphic art.
House At the Stone Bell (Dům U Kamenného Zvonu), Staroměstské náměstí 13, P. 1 – Old Town, next to Kinský Palace. Specializes in modern art.
City Library, Mariánské náměstí 1, P. 1 – Old Town, Exhibitions of modern art.
Czech Museum of Art, Husova 19-21, P. 1 – Old Town Exhibitions in a medieval setting.
Gallery of the City of Prague (Galerie hlavního města Prahy), Old Town Hall, P. 1 – Old Town. Exhibitions in the historical halls of the Town Hall (cloister and Knights' Hall).
Rudolphinum Gallery Alšovo nábřeží 12, P. 1 – Old Town.
Route: Metro Line A, Staroměstská station. Entrance on the embankment.
Royal Summer Palace (Královský letohrádek), Chotkovy sady, P. 1 – Hradčany. Exhibitions in the 16th century halls.
Ball-Games Court (Míčovna) in the Royal Garden of Prague Castle, P. 1 – Hradčany.
Imperial Stables (Královské konírny), Prague Castle.
Route: On the way to the Castle from the tram stop Hrad.

Mánes House of the Arts (Dům výtvarného umění Mánes), Masarykovo nábřeží 250, P. 1 – Nové Město, on the bank of the Vltava, exhibitions of modern art. Under reconstruction.
Josef Sudek Gallery (Galerie Josefa Sudka), Úvoz 24, P. 1
Prague House of Photography (Pražský dům fotografie), Husova 23, P. 1 – Old Town.
Vyšehrad Gallery (Vyšehradská galerie), Soběslavova 1, P. 2.

The Capital City of Prague has more than 30 theatres. They present a broad choice of performances ranging from opera and ballet to drama and modern forms.
Performances usually begin at 7 p. m. or 8 p. m. On Saturdays and Sundays matinés are given at 2 p. m. or 3 p. m. in some theatres. The theatres close down in July and August. Open-air performances and concerts are given in the summer season.
Advance ticket agencies:
Bohemia Ticket International, Salvátorská 6, P. 1 – Na Příkopě 16 - Karlova 8.
IFB Bohemia, Václavské náměstí 25, P. 1.
Tiketpro, Prague Information Centre, Staroměstské náměstí 22 – Na Příkopě 20, P. 1 – Lucerna, Štěpánská 61, Melantrich, Václavské náměstí 38 – AVČ, Main Station.
WOLFF, Na Příkopě 24, P. 1
Čedok, Na Příkopě 26, P. 1
During the main tourist season it is advisable that tickets be purchased in advance at ticket agencies or the theatre box office.

The National Theatre (Národní divadlo), Národní 2, P. 1
Route: Metro Line B, Národní třída station.
The Neo-Renaissance building stands on the bank of the R. Vltava by Legion Bridge (most Legií). It was festively inaugurated in 1883 as the centre of Czech striving for national independence and is to this day the main and most representative Czech theatre. The repertory includes opera, ballet and drama performances.

The State Opera Praha, Wilsonova 8, P. 2 – New Town.
Route: Metro Lines A and C, Muzeum station.
The building of the years 1886-88 stands on the North-South Freeway close to the Main Station.
Originally known as the German Theatre, The repertory includes mainly opera and ballet.

The Theatre of the Estates (Stavovské divadlo), Železná Street 11, P. 1 – Staré Město.
Route: Metro Lines A and B, Můstek station. Neo-Classical building 1781–1783, the first Czech performance given in 1785, belonged to the Bohemian Estates from 1799.

Kolowrat Theatre, Ovocný trh 6, P. 1 – Old Town.
Route: Metro Lines A and B, Můstek station.
Czech and foreign plays.

Theatres

The foyer
of the National Theatre

Laterna Magica, Národní 4, P. 1 – New Town.
Route: Metro Line B, Národní třída station.
Performances are given in the New Theatre next to the National Theatre. Combination of different elements: music, songs, living actors, dancers, film projection on differently sized screens. The Laterna Magica shows are easily understood and enjoy great popularity particularly among foreign visitors.

The Vinohrady Theatre (Divadlo na Vinohradech), náměstí Míru 7, P. 2 – Vinohrady
Route: Metro Line A, Náměstí Míru station. Art Nouveau building (1905–1909), close to the Church of St Ludmila (kostel sv. Ludmily) at Vinohrady. Drama performances with a richly varied repertory and a well-known cast.

The Drama Club (Činoherní klub), Ve Smečkách 26, P. 1 – Nové Město,
Route: Metro Lines A and C, Muzeum station. Holds performances close to Wenceslas Square. The repertory includes classical as well as modern authors.

The Music Theatre in Karlín (Hudební divadlo v Karlíně), Křižíkova 10, P. 8 –Karlín,
Route: Metro Lines B and C, Florenc station. Neo-Baroque building of 1891 (designed by F. Fellner and E. Helmer). Czech and world operettas and musicals.

The Theatre On the Ballustrade (Divadlo Na Zábradlí), Anenské náměstí 5, P. 1 – Staré Město.
Route: Metro Line A, Staroměstská station. Small theatre in a historic Old Town house. High quality performances of plays and mime of world renown.

The Spejbl and Hurvínek Theatre (Divadlo Spejbla a Hurvínka), Dejvická 38, P. 6.
Route: Metro Line A, Dejvická station. The best Czech puppet theatre.

The Reduta Theatre, Národní 20, P. 1 –Nové Město,
Route: Metro Line B, Národní třída station. Frequent guest performances by small theatres. Classical jazz performances.

Viola, Národní 7, P. 1 –Old Town.
Route: Metro Line B, Národní třída station.
Poetry and prose readings, literary and music performances. Theatre for one actor.

Ta Fantastika Theatre, Karlova 8, P. 1 –Old Town.
Route: Metro Line A, Staroměstská station.
In the Unitarium Hall. Performances of the Black Theatre and other modern theatre forms.

The Black Theatre of Jiří Srnec, Národní 40, P. 1 –New Town. Performances of the Black Theatre.

Theatre in Celetná Street, Celetná 17, P. 1 –Old Town. New forms.

Spiral Theatre (divadlo Spirale), Exhibition Grounds (Výstaviště), P. 7 –Holešovice.
Jesus Christ Superstar.

Theatres

Chamber Opera Prague –Opera Mozart, Novotného Lávka 1, P. 1 - Old Town. Performances on Mozartian motives.

National Marionette Theatre, Žatecká 1, P. 1 – Old Town. Marionette theatre for children and adults.

Concerts are an integral part of the broad kaleidoscope of cultural life in Prague. The town's music tradition goes back to the Middle Ages to church music and was continued by visits of world famous composers such as W. A. Mozart and L. van Beethoven and then the great Czech composers B. Smetana and A. Dvořák. The climax of the present music tradition in Prague is the Prague Spring Music Festival, which begins on 12 May, the day that Smetana died, and continues until early June. Musicians from many countries participate. This is followed by the Prague Cultural Summer Festival when the historic palaces, churches and gardens are the setting for concerts. The following are the main Prague concert halls:

Dvořák Hall of the Rudolfinum (Dvořákova síň), náměstí Jana Palacha, P. 1 – Old Town, where concerts are given by the Czech Philharmonic, its chamber ensembles and soloists.

Smetana Hall of the Municipal House (Smetanova síň Obecního domu), náměstí Republiky 5, P. 1 – Old Town. At present under reconstruction.

Josef Mánes Hall in St Agnes Convent (Síň Josefa Mánesa v Anežském klášteře), U milosrdných 17, P. 1 – Old Town, historic setting.

House At the Stone Bell (U kamenného zvonu), Staroměstské náměstí 13, P. 1 – Old Town.

Lichtenstein Palace, Malostranské náměstí 13, P. 1 – Malá Strana.

Nostitz Salon, Nostitz Palace, Maltézské náměstí, P. 1 – Malá Strana.

Bertramka, Mozartova 169, P. 5 –Smíchov.

The National Museum (Národní muzeum), Václavské náměstí 68, P. 1 – New Town.

St James' (kostel sv. Jakuba), **St Thomas'** (kostel sv. Tomáše), **St Nicholas'** (kostel sv. Mikuláše), **Our Lady at the Theatines** (kostel P. Marie u kajetánů), **St Francis'** (kostel sv. Františka), **St Ursula's** (kostel sv. Voršily) **St Michael's** (kostel sv. Michala), **Týn Church** (Týnský kostel) – organ concerts. **Wallenstein Garden** (Valdštejnská zahrada), **Garden on the Ramparts** (Zahrada Na Valech) – open-air concerts.

More than 300 cinemas are to be found on the territory of the capital city. The first-run cinemas in the centre of the city are very popular while there is less interest in the smaller cinemas in the suburbs. Admission tickets can be purchased a week ahead at the box offices or the advance booking offices. Performances usually begin at 10.30, 15, 17.30 and 20 hrs. Addresses of the main first-run cinemas:

Blaník, Václavské náměstí 56, P. 1 – Nové Město
Lucerna, Vodičkova 36, P. 1 – Nové Město
Světozor, Vodičkova 39, P. 1 – Nové Město
Pasáž, Václavské náměstí 5, P. 1 – Nové Město
Kino 64 –U hradeb, Mostecká 21, P. 1 – Malá Strana
Hvězda, Václavské náměstí 38, P. 1 – Nové Město

ENTERTAINMENT AND ENLIGHTENMENT

In the tourist season Prague offers a broad palette of performances, particularly in the following two places:

Exhibition Grounds (Výstaviště), P. 7, Metro Line C, Nádraží Holešovice station; large grounds in the former royal deer-park. In 1891 the Jubilee Exhibition was held here and the Industrial Palace dates from that time. The Brussels Pavilion represented Czechoslovakia at EXPO 58; pavilion of the City of Prague (Deposit of the National Museum), Sports Hall, swimming pool, panorama of the Battle of Lipany by painter L. Marold in a circular building of 1908 (open Tuesday-Sunday 10–16); a number of covered and open-air stages are used throughout the year for cultural programmes, exhibitions, fairground attractions, sports facilities. National and international exhibitions and trade-fairs are held throughout the year.

The Palace of Culture (Palác kultury), 5. května 65, P. 4 – Nusle. Vast six-storey building (1976–1981) with a number of large halls close to the Nusle Bridge; performances of plays, ballet, concerts, balls, films, programmes for children and youth, video-programmes. Used for congresses, conferences, international exhibitions.

Cabarets, Reviews, Night Clubs

Cabaret At the Fleks (U Fleků), Křemencova 9, P. 1 – Nové Město, Old Prague songs and chansons in the setting of a historic brewery.
Varieté Praga, Vodičkova 30, P. 1 – Nové Město; variety shows with international participation, from 21.30 hrs.
Revue Alhambra – Cold Fingers, Václavské náměstí 5, in the Ambassador Hotel, P. 1 – Nové Město, revue programmes, open 20.30–03 hrs.
Club Lávka, Novotného lávka 1, P. 1, by Charles Bridge.
Tatra Bar, Václavské náměstí, P. 1.
Eden-Palladium Dance Club, U Slavie, P. 10. The largest Disco in Prague.

Night Clubs:

Jazz concerts, Rock and Pop Music late into the night.
Bunkr, Lodecká 2, P. 1. Rock Club with frequent foreign performers.
Rock Café, Národní 20, P. 1. Concerts are followed by discos.
Prague Classic Club, Pařížská 4, P. 1. Classical rock music of the 60s and 70s.
Uzi Rock Bar, Legerova 44, P. 2. Music, juke boxes, video, disco.
Metropolitan Jazz Club, Jungmannova 14, P. 1. Jazz performances.
Reduta, Národní 28, P. 1. Classical jazz (Visited by the American President Bill Clinton).

---

*Entertainment
and Enlightenment*

Highlander, Národní 28, P. 1. Jazz club.
Esplanade – Est Bar, Washingtonova 19, P. 1. Live music.
Diplomat – Skyline Night club, Evropská 15, P. 6.
Radost FX, Bělehradská 120, P. 2. Techno-laser lights show.
Music Park, Francouzská 4, P. 2. Mega laser show.

Casinos:
Most casinos in Prague are open until 4 a. m. Roulette and Black Jack.
Casino Praha, Vinohradská 25, P. 2.
Casino Admiral in the Palace of Culture, 5. května 65, P. 4.
Casino Parkhotel, Veletržní 20, P. 7.
Casino de France, Hotel Atrium (Hilton), Pobřežní 3, P. 8.
Casino Palais Savarin, Na Příkopě 10, P. 1.
Casino Hotel Forum, Kongresová 4, P. 4.
Casino Hotel Ambassador, Václavské náměstí 5, P. 1.
Casino Tivoli, Náměstí Míru 18, P. 2.
Casino President, nám. Curieových 100, P. 1.
VIP Club Casino, Václavské náměstí 7, P. 1.

Enlightenment
The Petřín Observatory, P. 1; observation of the sky, astronomical programmes, exhitions, geography lectures.

Zoological Garden, Troja, P. 7; in an attractive natural setting on the right bank of the

R. Vltava and adjacent slopes with woodland, rocks, valleys; established 1931, area 45 ha, more than 600 species of animals, successful breeding of the Przewalski's horse, large reptile pavilion; parking place and restaurant at the entrance, in close proximity of chateau Troja, access by bus from Metro Line C, Nádraží Holešovice station.

Botanical Garden, Na slupi, P. 1 – Nové Město, established 1897, serves for botany studies of Charles University.

Planetarium, Královská obora 233, P. 7 close to the Exhibition Ground, built 1960–1962, in the dome, projection of the two hemispheres of the starry sky, popular scientific programmes, lectures.

SPORTS FACILITIES

Strahov Sports Grounds, in Prague 6 – Břevnov close to Petřín Hill above Smíchov. Access by bus from Dejvice (Metro Line A, Dejvická station), and from Smíchov. The largest building is the Stadium opened 1926 for the 8th All Sokol Sports Festival, where from 1955 Spartakiads were held every five years. One of the largest stadiums in the world, covering an area of 6 ha (200 x 300 m) Capacity: 220 000 spectators.In the eastern grandstand is a gymnasium and a swimming pool. Opposite the western grandstand is the Evžen Rošický stadium.

Sparta Praha Stadium, on Letná Heights (Metro Line A, Hradčanská station, used for football matches (30 000 spectators).

Slavia Praha Sports Grounds, Prague 10, Vršovice at Eden, covers an area of 30 ha, football stadium with athletics track, capacity: 41 000 spectators, further, winter stadium, sports hall; indoor and open-air swimming pools, etc.

Sports Hall in the Exhibition Grounds at Holešovice, Metro line C, Nádraží Holešovice station, originated in 1962 by reconstruction of one of the exhibition pavilions, venue of ice-hockey world championships, figure skating championships, sports gymnastics, table tennis, netball, handball, etc. Used for pop-music concerts, capacity: 18 500 spectators.

Central Tennis Court at Štvanice, on an island in the Vltava (Metro Line C, Vltavská station), modern tennis courts with covered training area, capacity of the central court: 7 000 spectators, venue of the Federation Cup (unofficial world championship of women's teams), Davis Cup matches.

Horse Race Track at Velká Chuchle, along the road to Strakonice, 12 km south of the centre, flat races, races over wicker hurdles and steeple chases are held every weekend from March until November.

Swimming Stadium in Podolí (plavecký stadion), Prague 4, access by tram in the

Sports facilities

direction of Braník; indoor pool 50 x 20 m, two outdoor pools (50 x 21 m and 33 x 21 m), diving tower.

Winter Stadiums (zimní stadióny): Štvanice (Prague 7), Sports Hall, side hall (P. 7), Slavia Praha IPS (P. 10).

Indoor Swimming Pools: Klárov (nábřeží kpt. Jaroše, P. 1), Exhibition Ground (P. 7), Radlice (P. 5), Motorlet sports ground, Slavia (P. 10, Slavia sports ground), ZPA Košíře (P. 5).

Lidos Lhotka (P. 4, lake), Motol (P. 5, lake), Šeberák (P. 4, lake, also nudist beach), Džbán (P. 6, valley reservoir, also nudist beach), Hostivař (P. 10 valley reservoir)

Golf: Motol (P. 5), behind Hotel Golf. 9 tees

Bicycle Rent: Půjčovna kol, Za humny 4, P. 6

Fitness Centres: Patenidis, Stodůlecká hala 0, Metro B Jinonice. Pohořelec, Dlabačov 1, P. 6. Body and Fitness Club, Bolzanova 7, P. 1.

Tennis: Clubhotel, Praha Průhonice, by motorway D1.

Squash: Fitness Centre Pohořelec, Štvanice, Sportcentrum Nové Butovice, Ovčí hájek 2174, P.5

Club Hotel, Praha Průhonice
Esque Squash Centrum, Strahov Stadium.

The Swimming Pool
in Podolí

The main axis of the public transport network is formed by the 3 lines of the **Prague Metro.** The rest of the town is serviced by **trams** and **buses,** which run through the centre in reduced numbers.

There is a flat rate for all means of public transport throughout Prague. The Metro uses the same tickets. Children to the age of 6 years use the entire transport network free of charge. Buses and trams are operated without conductors. Tickets are sold at all newspaper kiosks, tobacco shops, foodstores, in hotel reception offices, and ticket machines. The ticket must be punched in a little machine on entering the respective vehicle, or at the entrance to the Metro. Metro trains run from 5-24 hrs; at night special trams and buses run at 40 minute intervals. Tourists may purchase special passes for one or more days valid on all means of public transport.

Ask for detailed information.

Prague transport

Prague Metro:

Line **A** (green): Dejvická-Hradčanská-Malostranská-Staroměstská-Můstek-Muzeum-Náměstí Míru-Jiřího z Poděbrad-Flora-Želivského-Strašnická-Skalka; length: 10.1 km, time of travel 20 min.

Line **B** (yellow): Zličín-Stodůlky-Luka-Lužiny-Hůrka-Nové Butovice-Jinonická-Radlická-Nádraží Smíchov-Anděl-Karlovo náměstí-Národní třída-Můstek-Náměstí Republiky-Florenc-Křižíkova-Invalidovna-Palmovka-Českomoravská; length: 19.3 km, time of travel: 31 min.

Line **C** (red): Háje-Opatov-Chodov-Roztyly-Kačerov-Budějovická-Pankrác– Pražského povstání-Vyšehrad-I. P. Pavlova-Muzeum-Hlavní nádraží (Main Station)-Florenc-Vltavská-Nádraží Holešovice; length: 14.2 km, time of travel: 25 min.

Railway Transport:

Prague is the starting point of 10 railway lines; on its territory there is a total of 44 stations and stops. Seat reservations, berths in couchettes and sleeping cars can be booked at all larger stations (ARES system).

Prague Main Station (Praha – hlavní nádraží) in the centre of the city close to Wenceslas Square, Metro Line C station, Art Nouveau station building of 1901–1909, reconstructed 1980 with a modern concourse. Most international and national fast and through trains depart from the Main Station.

Masaryk Station (Masarykovo nádraží), in Hybernská Street, Metro Line B Náměstí Republiky station; the oldest Prague station dating back to 1845 with typical towers; fast and slow trains in the direction of Děčín, Chomutov, Pardubice, Brno, Bratislava depart from here.

Prague-Smíchov Station (Nádraží Praha – Smíchov). Metro Line B Nádraží Smíchov station, the building dates from 1952–1956; departure of trains (fast and slow) to West Bohemia.

Prague-Holešovice Station (Nádraží Praha – Holešovice), modern station close to the Metro Line C Nádraží Holešovice station, international trains in the direction of Berlín, Budapest and the Balkans, fast trains to Ústí n. L.

Bus Transport:

Bus routes link Prague with suburban townships (commuting services) and have their terminus by a Metro station or tram terminus on the edge of Prague. Most long-distance coaches (national and international) leave from the bus terminus Praha-Florenc (Metro Lines B and C, Florenc station), where seat reservations can be made and return tickets obtained. Other major bus terminuses can be found at the Metro Line C Roztyly station, at Smíchov (Metro Line B, Anděl station), in Dejvice (Metro LIne A, Hradčanská station), in Vysočany, in Strašnice (Metro Line A, Želivského station), in Holešovice (Metro Line C, Nádraží Holešovice).

Tickets and seat reservations: For international travel e. g. at the Bohemiatour travel agency, Zlatnická 7, P. 1 – Bohemia Euroexpress International, Koněvova 126, P. 3 – AC Tour, Opletalova 28, P. 1 and in the Čedok travel agency, Na Příkopě 18, P. 1.

Air Transport:

Airport Praha-Ruzyně, 15 km from the centre of the city (in the direction of Slaný), public transport buses go to the Metro Line A Dejvice station, Czechoslovak Airline (ČSA) coaches go to the air terminal in Revoluční Street near Šverma Bridge. Flight tickets and reservations can be obtained at the ČSA offices in Revoluční Street next to the Kotva department store. Ruzyně Airport built 1968 has to cope with growing air traffic. Observation terraces.

River transport:
The pier for steamships and motor boats is near Palacký bridge (Metro Line B, Karlovo náměstí station). In summer, according to the level of water, steamboats go up river to the Slapy Dam (4 hrs), motorboats downstream to the Zoo and Roztoky. Observation trips of Old Prague and evening dance parties on board are organized.

Cable-car:
The cable-car up Petřín Hill was inaugurated on the occasion of the Jubilee Exhibition in 1891. It was last reconstructed in 1985. The lower station is at Újezd, the middle station near the Nebozízek restaurant, the upper in the proximity of the Petřín View Tower. Tickets as in public transport. – In Prague Zoo a seat-lift is in operation.

Taxi:
A number of private firms provide taxi services. All taxis are marked and must have a functioning taxi-meter showing the tariff per kilometre, the distance covered and extra charges (e. g. at night). On request the driver will issue a receipt. It is advisable to inquire the cost before entering the taxi. Most taxi firms have a dispatcher through whom a taxi can be ordered by phone (Taxi Praha tel.: 2491 2344). Taxi ranks are to be found in frequented places.

Using your own car:
A valid driving licence, car papers (or proof of a rented car) and a green card of international insurance are required. Safety belts must be used also in the towns. There is a 100 % prohibition of the consumption of alcohol for the driver. speed limit: in towns and villages 60 km, on the open road 90 km, on the motorway 110 km. Orientation in Prague is difficult for those who do not live here in view of one-way streets and pedestrian zones. Parking is restricted with some facilities near the Main Station and on Charles Square. Underground parking facilities near the Rudolfinum and the National Theatre. It is strongly recommended that no valuables, passport and other documents and money be left in the vehicle, which should be well locked and have a security system.

MONEY

Money Exchange
The majority of big banks of the Czech Republic have branches in Prague where exchange offices are open Monday to Friday from 8 a. m. to 4 p. m. Some are open on Saturdays. Banks like the Komerční banka, Živnostenská Banka, Obchodní banka are situated in Na Příkopě street and in the vicinity. In recent years a dense network of exchange offices has been opened in all areas frequented by foreign tourists. 24 hour service is provided by the Chequepoint exchange offices in ulice 28. října 13, Staroměstské náměstí 21, Vodičkova 41. Most of the others are open from 8.30 a. m. – 10.30 p. m. The American Express exchange office is situated on Wenceslas Square (Václavské náměstí 56), open 9 a. m. – 8 p. m., Saturday 9 a. m. to 3 p. m. Major foreign banks likewise have

---

Money

branches in Prague: ABN AMRO Bank (Revoluční 1), Bank Austria (Revoluční 15), Deutsche Bank (Jungmannova 34), Raiffeisenbank (Vodičková 38), Citibank (Evropská 178), Credit Suisse (Staroměstské náměstí 15), Bayerische Vereinsbank (Italská 24), Dresdner Bank (Opletalova 25), and others.

Currency
The unit of currency of the Czech Republic is the **Czech Crown** – koruna (Kč) 1 Kč = 100 Heller). The following banknotes are in circulation: 5 000, 1 000, 500, 200, 100, 50 and 20 Crowns. These coins are in use: 50, 20, 10, 5, 2, 1 Kč and 50, 20 and 10 Heller coins. As of 1995 the Czech Crown is freely convertible. It can be taken abroad and exchanged for other currencies.
There is a growing network of stores and restaurants where credit cards are accepted (chiefly American Express, VISA, Master Cards and Access). Automatic teller machines have been installed in certain places.

ACCOMMODATION

With the growth in tourism the number of hotels, pensions and private accommodation has increased, and the quality is improving. Prices correspond to those in other European cities. Certain facilities are fully booked for group travel, others provide accommodation only when arranged through a travel agency. It is recommended that accommodation in the town centre and in the main season be booked well in advance.

Five-Star Hotels
Esplanade, Washingtonova 19, P. 1. Tel.: 2421 1715, Fax: 2422 9306.
Inter-Continental, náměstí Curieových 43, P. 1. Tel.: 2488 1111, Fax: 2488 0123. With a view of the Old Town and Prague Castle.
Jalta, Václavské náměstí 45, P. 1. Tel.: 2422 9133, Fax: 2421 3866.
Palace, Panská 12, P. 1 Tel.: 2409 3111, Fax: 2422 1240. One of the most luxurious hotels in the city centre.
Penta Renaissance, V celnici 1, P. 1. Tel.: 2481 0396, Fax: 231 31 33. modern hotel.
Praha, Sušická 20, P. 6. Tel.: 2434 2614, Fax: 312 1757. Situated in a quiet villa district.
Paříž, U Obecního domu 1, P. 1. Tel.: 2422 2151, Fax: 2422 5475. Built in Art Nouveau style, listed as monument.
Savoy, Keplerova 6-8, P. 6. Tel.: 2451 0989, Fax: 2430 2128. Close to Prague Castle.

Four-Star Hotels:
Atlantic, Na Poříčí 9. Tel.: 2481 1084, Fax: 2481 2378.
Barcelo Praha, Na Strži 32, P. 4. Tel.: 692 2850, Fax: 692 2857.
City Hotel Moráň, Na Moráni 15, P. 2. Tel.: 24 91 52, Fax: 29 75 33.
Diplomat, Evropská 15, P. 6. Tel.: 2439 4111, Fax: 34 17 31. A large modern hotel near Metro station Dejvická (Line A).
Forum, Kongresová 4, P. 4. Tel.: 6119 1111, Fax: 42 06 84. High-rise building by Nusle Bridge in the vicinity of the Palace of Culture.

Hilton-Atrium, Pobřežní 1, P. 8. Tel.: 2484 1111, Fax: 2481 1896. A large modern hotel.
Hoffmeister, Pod Bruskou 9, P. 1. Tel.: 2451 0381, Fax: 53 09 59. A small cosy hotel at the foot of Prague Castle.
Olympik, Sokolovská 138, P. 8. Tel.:6618 1111, Fax: 6631 0559.
Panorama, Milevská 7, P. 4. Tel.: 6116 1111, Fax.: 42 62 63.
Parkhotel, Veletržní 20, P. 7. Tel.: 3807 1111, Fax: 38 20 10. In the vicinity of the Exhibition Grounds.
President, Náměstí Curieových 100, P. 1, Tel.: 231 48 12, Fax: 231 82 47. On the bank of the R. Vltava in the Old Town.
U tří pštrosů, Dražického náměstí, P. 1. Tel.: 2451 0779, Fax: 2451 0783. A small cosy hotel by Charles Bridge.
Don Giovanni, Vinohradská, P. 3. Tel.: 67 03 67 03, Fax: 67 03 67 04. close to Metro station Želivského, Line A.
Villa Voyta, K Novému dvoru, P. 4. Tel.: 472 55 11, Fax: 472 94 26.
Meteor Plazza, Hybernská 6, P. 1. Tel.: 2419 2130, Fax: 2421 3005.
Club Hotel Praha, Průhonice. Tel.: 643 65 01, Fax: 643 67 73. By motorway D 1.

Three-Star Hotels:
Albatros, (Botel – Hotel on a Boat) Nábřeží L. Svobody. Tel.: 2481 0547 Fax: 2481 1214.
Andanta, Ve smečkách 4, P. 1. Tel.: 2423 0888, Fax: 264 391.
Atlantic, Na poříčí 9, P. 1. Tel.: 2481 1083, Fax: 24 81 23 78.
Evropa, Václavské náměstí 25, P. 1. Tel.: 2422 8117, Fax: 2422 4544.
Harmony, Na poříčí 31, P. 1. Tel.: 232 0720, Fax: 231 0009.
International, Koulova 15, P. 6. Tel.: 2439 3111, Fax: 2431 0616.
Juliš, Václavské náměstí 22, P. 1. Tel.: 2421 7092, Fax: 2421 8545.
Kampa, Všehrdova 16, Tel.: 2451 0408, Fax: 2451 0377.
Karl-Inn, Šaldova 54, P. 8. Tel.: 2481 1718, Fax: 2481 2681.
Pyramida, Bělohorská 214, P. 6. Tel.: 311 32 96, Fax: 311 3291. close to Prague Castle.
Splendid, Ovenecká 33, P. 7. Tel.: 375 451.
Vondra, Na Břevnovské pláni 73, P. 6. Tel.: 355 505, Fax: 362 263. Quiet situation.

Two-Star Hotels:
Axa, Na poříčí 40, P. 1. Tel.: 2481 2580, Fax: 232 21 72.
Franta, Ohradské náměstí 5, P. 5. Tel.: 561 55 57, Fax: 561 55 56.
Juniorhotel, Žitná 12, P. 2. Tel.: 2491 57 67, Fax: 249 948.
Juventus, Planická 10, P. 2. Tel.: 255 151, Fax: 255 153.
Vítkov, Koněvova 114, P. 3. Tel.: 279 341, Fax: 279 357.
A large number of pensions have opened in recent years, mostly situated in the suburbs of Prague. They provide accommodation in reasonable comfort in a more personal setting. Full board is often provided. Adresses and prices can be obtained from the following travel agencies:
Pragotour – PIS, Za Poříčskou branou 7, P. 8. Tel.: 26 35 43, Fax: 2422 8557.
Toptour, Rybná 3, P. 1. Tel.: 269 65 26, Fax: 2481 1400.
Čedok, Panská 5, P. 1. Tel.: 2421 4192.
AVE, Main Station, P. 1. Tel.: 2422 3226, Fax: 2422 3463.
AVE, Ruzyně Airport, Tel.: 334 31 06.

Accommodation

The international four star hotel offers its top quality service in 413 double rooms and 20 suits. You can have your meal either at luxurious restaurant Crystal or at buffet restaurant Moravia offering nice and pleasant atmosphere or at fast-food center called Aperitiv bar, cafe Split with outdoor terrace or finally in the night-club Disco. On the 24th floor you can find the swimming pool with bar, sauna, solarium and you can have your massage here.

The conference rooms with the capacity of as many as 350 persons are suitable for holding the seminars, lectures and festival events.

Panorama hotel will be happy to welcome you!

HOTEL
PANORAMA
a. s.
Milevská 7
140 00 Praha 4
Tel.: 0042-2-6116 1111
Fax: 0042-2-42 62 63
Telex: 0042-2-123576

Member of
TOP
International
Hotels'

Hostels:
Cheap accommodation is provided in tourist hostels and, during the summer months, in student halls of residence. The Juniorhotel in Žitná street 12 is included in the network of hostels (Tel.: 2422 3226, Fax: 2422 3463).
The largest Prague hostel, especially for young people, is Strahov-ESTEC, Vaníčkova 5/block 5, P. 6, in the halls of residence. Tel.: 521 250, Fax: 527 343.

Campsites:
Aritma Džbán, Nad lávkou 8, P. 6. Tel.: 368 551, Fax: 361 365. Approach along the road from the airport.
Troja, Trojská 157, P. 8. Tel.: 84 28 33. Direction ZOO.
Kotva Braník, U ledáren 55, P. 4. Tel.: 46 13 97.
Sportcamp Motol and **Caravancamp Motol,** V podhájí, P. 5. along the road to Plzeň.

CATERING FACILITIES

There is a wide offer of catering facilities with a broad range in price and quality. Hotel guests usually have breakfast included in the room charge, often in buffet form. Breakfast is served from 7–9 a. m., lunch between 11.30 a. m. and 2.30 p. m., supper (dinner), around 7 p. m. Many restaurants serve hot meals all day. Menu-cards in English, German, at times French or Italian, are provided in restaurants frequented by foreign visitors. The offer includes traditional dishes of the Czech cuisine (pork with sauerkraut or breaded pork steak with potato salad). Dumplings are typical with many dishes. Soup (potato, vegetable, mushroom or consommé) is served at lunchtime. Sausages, goulash, meat in a sauce, with dumpling, rice or potatoes are also popular. Desserts include omelettes, buns, cake or apfelstrudel. Preference is given to rye bread or to a variety of rolls. Typical beverages are the various Czech beers (Prague Staropramen, Pilsen Urquell, Gambrinus from Plzeň, Budvar from České Budějovice, Radegast from Nošovice). Czech wines come from Mělník and Litoměřice, while the largest vineyards are to be found in the south of Moravia, near the border with Slovakia and Austria. The best-known Czech liqueur is Becherovka, made of different herbs to a secret recipe. The best-known spirits are Slivovice and Borovička. Coffee is often drunk black.
Prague has a choice of national restaurants (Chinese, Vietnamese, Indian, Italian, French, Greek) with a broad offer of beverages. Prices of food and drink are lower in Prague than in Western Europe. The highest prices are charged close to tourist centres, especially in the vicinity of the Old Town Square, Wenceslas Square, in the Lesser Town (Malá Strana) and at the Castle. Prices are lower away from these areas. In the suburbs beer and cold cuts tend to be on offer.
The following list includes catering facilities that are recommended to foreign tourists in view of the special offers, interesting situation, gastronomical specialities. There exist, of course, far more restaurants, quality and offer may change, and new catering facilities are constantly coming into existence.
It is the custom that a tip amounting to 5–10 % of the price of the meal is added.

Catering
facilities

Restaurants:
Alex, Revoluční 11, P. 1. German and international cuisine.
Asia, Letohradská 50, P. 7. Asian cuisine.
Bellevue, Smetanovo nábřeží 18, P. 1.
Bohemia, Václavské náměstí 29, P. 1. Czech cuisine.
Chicago, Štěpánská 63, P. 1. Interior in the style of the 30s.
Cchang-Ccheng – Long Wall, Pujmanové 1218/10, P. 4. Chinese cuisine.
Hanau Pavilion, Letenské sady 173, P. 7. Good view.
Lví dvůr (Lions' Court), U Prašného mostu 6, P. 1.
Mayur, Štěpánská 61, P. 1. Indian restaurant.
Na Příkopě, Na příkopě 16, P. 1. Czech cuisine.
Nebozízek, Petřinské sady 411, P. 1. View of Prague.
Peklo, Strahovské nádvoří 1, P. 1. Vaulted rooms below Strahov Abbey.
Premiera, V Jirchářích 6, P. 1. French cuisine.
Restaurant Marie Theresia, Na příkopě 23, P. 1. Czech Cuisine.
Sakura, Štefánikova 7, P. 5. Japanese restaurant.
Shalom, Maiselova 18, P. 1. Kosher restaurant.
Trattoria Viola, Národní 7, P. 1. Italian cuisine.
U bílého koníka, Karlova 7, P. 1.
U Císařů, Loretánská 175, P. 1.
U Černé Dory, Masná 8, P. 1.
U červeného kola, Anežská 2, P. 1.
U Golema, Maiselova 8, P. 1.
U labutí, Hradčanské náměstí 11, P. 1. Czech cuisine.
U Lorety, Loretánské náměstí 8, P. 1.
U modré kachničky, Nebovidská 6, P. 1.
U Mecenáše, Malostranské náměstí, P. 1.
U staré synagogy, Pařížská 17, P. 1. Czech cuisine.
U sv. Salvatora, Staroměstské náměstí 7, P. 1. Czech cuisine.
U zlatých andělů, Celetná 29, P. 1. Czech cuisine.
Valdštejnská hospoda, Valdštejnské náměstí 7, P. 1.
Vltava, Rašínovo nábřeží 2, P. 1. On the bank of the R. Vltava. Fish specialities.
Zlatý drak, Anglická 6, P. 2. Chinese restaurant.
McDonalds' restaurants are to be found: Vodičkova 15, Václavské náměstí 9, Václavské náměstí 59, Sokolovská 54, Plzeňská 5, Mostecká 21, There are snack-cars and self-service restaurants in many places (e. g. Kentucky Fried Chicken and others).

Ale-Houses:
There are dozens of ordinary 3rd and 4th category ale-houses in Prague, visitors wishing to drink good beer in a period setting can select from the following:
U Fleků (At the Fleks'), Křemencova 9, P. 1; the brewery was established in 1459; it sells 13^0 dark beer, remarkable Neo-Gothic setting, garden with arcades
U Tomáše (At Thomas's), Letenská 12, P. 1; a brewery was established here in 1358, vaulted basement halls, dark 12^0 Braník beer
U kalicha (At the Chalice), Na bojišti 13, P. 2, inn made famous by J. Hašek's hero, the Good Soldier Schweik; Pilsner Urquell 12^0, house specialities, period decorations
U Schnellů (At the Schnells'), Tomášská 2, P. 1; ale-house with a good cuisine and 12^0

GRIL
RESTAURANT

Tkalcovský dvůr

U Lužického semináře 28
118 00 Praha 1 – Malá Strana

*Nice place in a stylish environment,
in a garden restaurant and a terrace*

●

*Chicken speciality made on the grill
Popular selection of Moravian wines
Prague beer „Staropramen" light and dark*

●

THANK'S FOR YOUR VISIT!

Pilsner Urquell beer, close to Malostranské náměstí

U Pinkasů (At the Pinkases'), Jungmannovo náměstí 15, P. 1, traditional restaurant with Pilsner Urquell beer; this was the place where it was first tapped in Prague

U Medvídků (At the Little Bears), Na Perštýně 7, P. 1, Budweiss Beer 12°

U dvou koček (At the Two Cats), Uhelný trh 10, P. 1, 12° Pilsner Urquell

Branický sklípek (Braník Cellar), Vodičkova 26, P. 1, Braník beer (even 14°)

Černý pivovar (Black Brewery), Karlovo náměstí 15, P. 2, 12° Pilsner Urquell

U zlatého tygra (At the Golden Tiger), Husova 17, P. 1 Pilsner Urquell 12°

U kocoura (At the Tom-Cat's) Nerudova 2, P. 1, 12° Pilsner Urquell

U Bonaparta (At Bonaparte's) Nerudova 29, P. 1, Staropramen 12° beer

U černého vola (At the Black Ox), Loretánské náměstí 1, P. 1, Velké Popovice 12° beer

U malvaze, Karlova 10, dark Braník beer

Novoměstský pivovar, Vodičkova 20, P. 1. Produces beer on the premises

U Vejvodů, Jilská 4, P. 1. Staropramen 12°

Coffee-Houses: The oldest Prague coffee-house was opened in the early 18th century in the House At the Three Ostriches (U tří pštrosů) in the Lesser Town. In the 19th and 20th centuries some of the coffee-houses were the meeting places of leading artists (e. g. the **Slávia** coffee-house opposite the National Theatre). A favourite meeting place is the Lesser Town coffee-house (**Malostranská kavárna**) on Malostranské náměstí.

Amadeus/Kamenný stůl, Staroměstské náměstí 18

Antik, Provaznická 1, P. 1

The At the Fleks' ale-house

Café Nouveau, Náměstí Republiky 5, P. 1
Puškin Café, Husova 14, P. 1
Savoy Café, Vítězná 1, P. 1
Columbia Café, Mostecká 3, P. 1
E.-E. Kisch Café, Celetná 2, P. 1
Týn Café, Staroměstské náměstí 5, P. 1
Vikárka, Vikářská 39, Prague Castle, P. 1

Wine Cellars: The most attractive are the wine-cellars in the basements of medieval Prague houses in the Old Town. Even demanding visitors will be satisfied with the selection of Moravian, Slovakian and sometimes Czech and foreign wines on offer.
Klášterní vinárna (Convent Wine Tavern), Národní 8, P. 1.
Svatá Klára (St Clara), U trojského zámku 9, P. 7; cellars by the vineyards close to the Zoo.
Lobkovická vinárna, Vlašská 17, P. 1
U černého slunce (At the Black Sun), Kamzíkova 9, P. 1
U Kolovrata, Valdštejnská 18, P. 1
U Malířů (At the Painters'), Maltézské náměstí 11, P. 1
U Markýze (At the Marquis'), Nekázanka 8, P. 1
U pavouka (At the Spider's), Celetná 17, P. 1
U tří zlatých Hvězd (At the Three Golden Stars), Malostranské náměstí 10, P. 1.

SHOPPING

Shopping facilities abound in the centre of Prague and in particular in the pedestrian zones, where there are department stores, specialized stores and small boutiques. Most shops are open from 9 a. m. to 6 p. m. Saturdays until 1 p. m. Some food shops open already at 6 or 7 a. m. The department stores offer a wide range of goods: **Kotva** on náměstí Republiky, **Máj** at the corner of Národní and Spálená, **Bílá Labuť** (White Swan) on Na poříčí street, on Václavské náměstí **Krone** and **Bílá Labuť.**
Bohemian glass and **porcelain,** popular with foreign visitors, can be purchased in many places, e. g. Národní 19 and 43, Staroměstské náměstí 26-27, Na příkopě 12, Karlova 14.
Folk art, e. g. wooden toys, dolls in national costume, painted Easter eggs, wicker-work, is on sale in shops on Národní 36, Karlova 23, Železná 16, Husova 12 and elsewhere. In the centre are numerous bookshops offering maps, guidebooks, illustrated books on Prague (e. g. Na Příkopě 3, Václavské náměstí 43, Na Příkopě 31). Food specialities can be found in shops on Jungmannovo náměstí, Národní, Na Příkopě. A big supermarket is situated between ulice 28. října and Rytířská streets. (Pronto S).
On Charles Bridge are stalls with art work and souvenirs. In the main tourist season street stalls and salesmen offer a variety of commodities, (including left-over Soviet army caps, uniforms and medals). The picturesque market on Havelská street in the Old Town offers a selection of vegetables, fruit and other foodstuffs. The largest market in Prague is situated on the premises of the one-time abattoir in Holešovice. Here a broad range of goods is offered at advantageous prices. The market-hall at Vinohrady is reserved for luxury articles.

Shopping

Information Service: PIS (Prague Information Service) Na příkopě 20, Tel.: 54 44 44 – Staroměstské náměstí, Tel.: 2421 2845. ČEDOK, Na příkopě 18, Tel.: 2419 7111. Welcome Touristic Prague Klimentská 2, P. 1, Tel.: 231 4661 – Premiant City Tour, Mostecká 21, P. 1, Tel.: 533 684.
City Tours: Depart from náměstí Republiky, Národní, Na příkopě, Organized by PIS, Čedok, Martin Tour (Štěpánská 61, Tel.: 2421 2473), IFB (Václavské náměstí 27, Tel.: 2422 7253), Novum Tour (náměstí Republiky 5, Tel.: 232 65 60). Every hour the "Ekoexpres"

The Kotva
department store

leaves from the Old Town Square (Staroměstské náměstí), for the Lesser Town (Malá Strana) and Prague Castle. In the main tourist season a historic tram, No. 91, goes through the inner city at weekends. Horse-drawn carriages can be hired on the Old Town Square.

Police: Konviktská 14, P. 1. Tel.: 158. Traffic accidents, Tel.: 773 455.
Emergency Medical Service: Tel.: 155. first aid: from 4.00 p. m. to 7. 00 a. m. Palackého 5, P. 1, Tel.: 2422 2520. – Sokolská 27, P. 2, Tel.: 299 676 – Dukelských hrdinů 1, P. 7, Tel.: 382 324. First aid for children at the same addresses. Dental emergency service Vladislavova 22, P. 1, Tel.: 2422 7663 (7.00 p. m. – 7.00 a. m.) (To be moved to Palackého 5).
Fire Brigade: (in case of fire, road accidents, floods) Tel.: 150.
Lost Property: Karoliny Světlé 5, P. 1 (Objects), Tel.: 236 88 87; Documents: Tel.: 278 551-4.
Customs: Sokolovská 22, P. 8. Tel.: 2421 9186
Car Repairs: Limuzská 12, P. 10, Tel.: 77 34 55 (round the clock emergency services); Pragis Assistance, Tel.: 75 81 15 (24 hr service); "Yellow Angel" Autoturist, Tel.: 154.
Car Rental American Express, Václavské náměstí 56, P. 1. Tel.: 2421 5397
Hertz, Karlovo náměstí 28, P. 2, Tel.: 299 237
EUROPcar, Pařížská 26, P. 1, Tel.: 24 81 0515
Rent-a-Car, Opletalova 33, P. 1, Tel.: 2421 1587
Avis, E. Krásnohorské 9, P. 1, Tel.: 231 55 15
Koospol Servis, Evropská 178, P. 6, Tel.: 316 52 04

A FEW CZECH TERMS TO HELP YOU FIND THE WAY ABOUT THE TOWN

---

chrám	church, cathedral	náměstí	square
divadlo	theatre	obchod	shop
hrad	castle	park	park
klášter	monastery, convent	prodejna	shop
kostel	church	stanice	stop (tram, bus)
město	town	třída	road, street
most	bridge	ulice	street
nádraží	station (railway, bus)	zahrada	garden

INDEX

OLYMPIA GUIDE

PRAGUE

brief guide

MARCEL LUDVÍK
SOŇA SCHEINPFLUGOVÁ
JOSEF ŠKVOR

English translation by PhDr. Till Gottheinerová
Photographs: Jiří Doležal, Jiří Kopřiva, Miroslav Krob,
Dalibor Kusák, Josef Molín, František Přeučil
Maps and plans by ing. Zdeněk Stehlík
Olympia Publishing House, Praha, 1996
Publication No. 2809
3rd edition, 132 pages
Editor: Marcela Nováková
Technical editor: Jan Zoul
Printed by Naše Vojsko, Praha
27-012-96

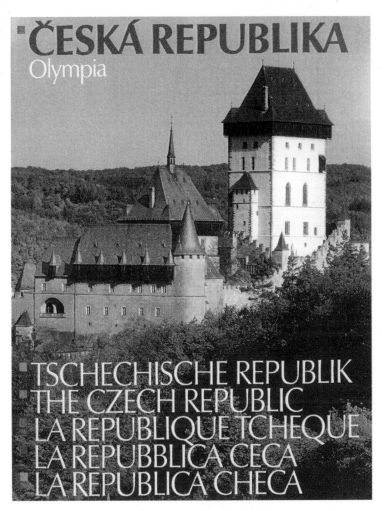

ČESKÁ REPUBLIKA
Olympia

TSCHECHISCHE REPUBLIK
THE CZECH REPUBLIC
LA REPUBLIQUE TCHEQUE
LA REPUBBLICA CECA
LA REPUBLICA CHECA

OBRAZOVÉ PUBLIKACE
BILDERBÜCHER
PHOTOGRAPHY BOOKS
PUBLICATIONS EN PHOTOS
PUBBLICAZIONI FOTOGRAFICHE
PUBLICATIONES EN FOTOGRAFÍAS

OLYMPIA

via

© Kartografie Praha, 1996

HRADČANY

KRÁLOVSKÁ ZAHRADA

Pražský hrad

JELENÍ PŘÍKOP

Jelení

MHU

108 - 132 - 143
149 - 174 - 180 - 216 - 217

Prašného mostu

22

Mariánské hradby

Míčovna

U Prašného mostu

Jízdárna
Pražského hradu

Jelení

U Brusnice

Jelení

Brusnice

JELENÍ PŘÍKOP

U Brusnice

ZAHRADA NA VALECH

LE

Nový Svět

Černínská

27

2

Na
náspu

P. Maria
Andělská

Klášter
kapucínů

sv. Jan
Nepomucký

Kapucínská

Šternberský
palác

Nár.
gal.

ZAHR.
NA
BAŠTĚ

ZAHRADA NA VALECH

U Prašné
studně

Valdšte

Kanc.
Post. sn

GB

W.

Churchill.

Šnemovní

Hudební
pavilón

Loreta

Ministerstvo
zahr. věcí

Loretánské
nám.

U kasáren

Martinický
palác

Arcibiskupský
palác

Hradčanské
nám.

sv. Benedikt

Vojen. hist.
muz.

Ke Hradu

46

Radnické
schody

P. Maria

Nerudova

2

IT

RO

18

Malostranské
nám.

sv. Mikuláš

TAXI

Loretánská

Pohořelec

44

Úvoz

11

32

Úvoz

zákl. šk.

47

Jánská

Šporkova

33

Jiřská

Lichtenštejnský
palác

AMU

Břetislavova

DE

20

Vlašská

7

Rubin

Tržiště

29

Prokop

Karmelit

SE

15

Nemocnice
sv. Karla
Boromejského

sv. Karel
Boromejský

34

21

VE

Schönbornský
palác

US

Schönbornská
ZAHRADA

VRTBOVSKÁ
ZAHRADA

22

Lobkovický
palác

Vlašská

42

25

Strahovský
klášter

Strahovské
nádvoří

P. Maria

44

27

LOBKOVICKÁ
ZAHRADA

J. Vrchlický

SCHÖNBORNSKÁ
ZAHRADA

zákl.
šk.

P. Maria
Vítězná

MŠMT

STRAHOVSKÁ
ZAHRADA

Petřínská
rozhledna

MALÁ STRANA

SPŠ
grafická

20

12 - 22 - 57

1 45

Strahovská

Hladová zeď

přír. pam.
Petřínské skalky

Academie
bludiště

kaple Božího hrobu
(Kalvárie)

stud.
Petřínka

SEMINÁŘSKÁ
ZAHRADA

Hellichova

13

7

Úřad

sv. Vavřinec

PETŘÍN

F. Laub

J. Neruda

U lanové
dráhy

VELKÝ
STRAHOVSKÝ
STADIÓN

132 - 143

149

Vaníčkova

217

Olympijská

Chaloupeckého

Jezdecká

6

Jezdecká

Šermířská

Praha 6

327

RŮŽOVÝ
SAD

M.R. Štefánik

Štefánikova
hvězdárna

lanová dráha

Nebozízek

V. Novák

K.H. Mácha

Hladová zeď

TJ Sokol
Malá Strana

KVĚTNICE

Úvoz

Rošic-
kých

náměs
Kinsky

sv. Michal

KINSKÉHO ZAHRADA

176

Hořejškova

19

Drtinova

Kroftova

Labyrint

Štefánikova

5a

Na Hřebenkách

62

176

2

35

U Plátenice

27

zahr. osada

5

skleník

zákl. škola
pro sluch. post.

letohrádek
Kinských

H. Kvapilová

25

Zubatého

14

29

3

U Nesypky

12

19

Tichá

4

Praha 5

VN

176

Hořejškova

Rak. škola
v Praze

AT

Viktora Huga

Svédska

U Nesypky

22

sv. Gabriel

31

býv. klášter
Sacré Coeur

základní
škola

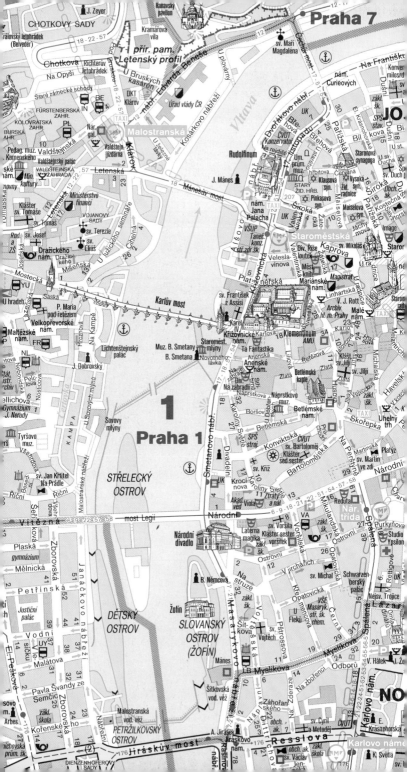

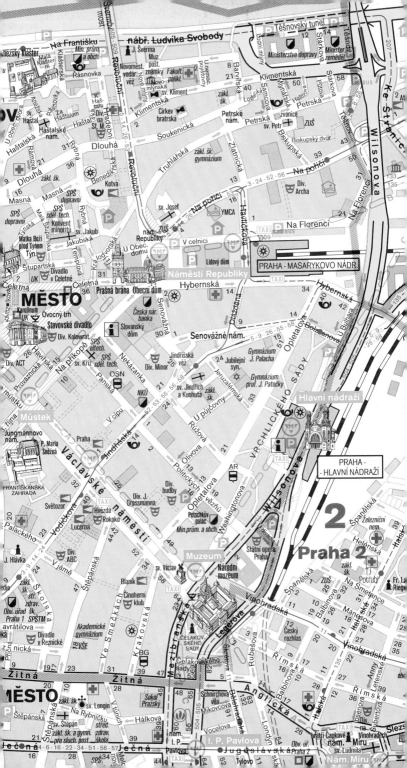